TEETH

An Oral History

JOHN PATRICK HIGGINS

Sagging Shorts

Printed in the United States of America.
Set in Mrs Eaves XL with LaTeX.

ISBN: 978-1-952386-82-4 (paperback)
ISBN: 978-1-952386-83-1 (ebook)
Library of Congress Control Number: 2023949160

Sagging Meniscus Press
Montclair, New Jersey
saggingmeniscus.com

For Susan, whose smile makes it all worthwhile

"Hair is the first thing. And teeth the second. A man got those two things, he's got it all."
—*James Brown*

Fillings

TEETH

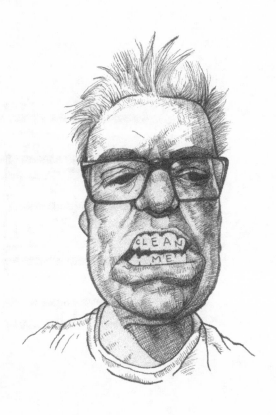

No, seriously, clean me

DOWN IN THE MOUTH
WITH JOHN PATRICK HIGGINS

———————◆———————

EETH, MORE THAN EYES, are the windows to the soul. You can be fit, conventionally good-looking, have lustrous hair and fine, firm limbs, but if you flash a snaggle-toothed smile—it's game over, man. You're a wrong 'un.

If your teeth are dirty, or broken, or missing or an unusual colour, it's because you're bad. You're a sloven. You have failed to maintain the upkeep of yourself. You very likely don't wash your hands when you use the toilet, and, for the love of all that's holy, please keep your genitals downwind. How hard is it to run a brush over your pearlies a couple of times a day, after all?

Bad teeth are a social failing too. They're what accents used to be—a dead giveaway. You can present yourself any way you choose, hit the gym, get some decent tailoring, but if you have bad teeth, it's all for nothing.

Bad teeth are proof of degeneracy. They're a slip, a tell, a badge of corruption. Bad teeth signify evil.

We all know this. Look at the oral furniture of witches, trolls or Dickensian footpads. Stained and broken and scattered round the gums like a poorly maintained rockery, bad teeth feature in the smiles of the unlettered, the thuggish, the bestial, the criminally insane. Every cinematic madman you've ever seen has laughed like an ape, flashing filthy fangs, long ropes of saliva hanging down like glistening bunting. In the episode of the TV show *Hammer House of Horror*, "The Two Faces of Evil", a man's murderous doppelganger is betrayed chiefly by his rotting teeth. It makes no sense—there's no reason for his sudden lapse in oral hygiene—it's used here as a marker of strangeness, of the uncanny. He looks like your husband, until he smiles his Brighton Beach smile, and then he's revealed to be *other*. In *Valerie and her Week of Wonders*, Valerie's wholesome father—a moustachioed Ed Sheeran lookalike—is revealed to be the vampiric Weasel, his white face contrasting with his long, verminous teeth.

The Covid Pandemic impacted the world in many ways, almost all of them terrible. People died, businesses went bust, we discovered people we loved and trusted were, at best, selfish arseholes, at worst delusional idiots. But for me, the upside was getting to wear a mask over my pub piano teeth. For two years I strutted around, confident no one knew I had a gobful of broken biscuits. In my nice coat and stylish shoes, I cut a rather dapper figure, not sliding into any obvious socio-economic group. Floating by. When wearing my mask, no one could discern the palpable evil of my rotting smile. I walked among you, frictionless, unplaceable.

My dad was nicknamed "Crocodile" when he was young. He had mouth like a Swiss Army knife: a tooth for everything. He had one for getting a stone out of a horse's hoof. It was a mouth that would have taken twenty years to grow into and, in fact, he never did. By the time I came along those teeth were a memory, replaced by neatly moulded dentures. He may have had some teeth left— there was a forlorn, splayed, brown-handled toothbrush in the bathroom, never replaced in my childhood. But I don't know, maybe he used it to clean his denture-plate, lifting spinach from the copper wiring.

It was the habit, in the past, for newly married couples to have all their teeth pulled and replaced by dentures. Teeth were troublesome, fallible things, prone to cracking, falling out or causing excruciating pain. Better to spend your wedding money getting rid of the filthy things and having them replaced by safe, reliable plastic. It's wipe-clean and it lasts a lifetime, if you don't smile too near the fire. I wonder how many honeymoons were spent spitting blood onto the pillow and sipping copper-tasting soup? However, I don't think that's what happened with my dad—he lost his teeth because he had crap teeth. They were large, weak, splintering things, crumbling like aspirin.

And those are the teeth I've inherited.

To be fair to me, most of my teeth are still in there. They've lasted half a century, which isn't bad going. I have no decay either. Dentists always compliment me on that, as they roll their little lollypop mirrors over the grey, crenulated ruins in my mouth, the teeth like an aquarium's coral castle, the fish long dead. My teeth are clean, but they look awful. Seriously, there may be lichen on them. They're like neolithic stones. It's all I can do to keep druids from camping out on my tongue each solstice.

I look at my teeth and despair. The front four, upper, are fine. That's because the front four, upper, are capped. There is another sarcastically white crown, lower right. It sits there like last house standing in a Blitzed terrace, a gleaming freak in the rubble. The rest of my teeth are low and sharp, hollow and stained. I have a mouth full of wet autumn leaves and loose chippings. I wouldn't even have the capped teeth but for a violent mugging. A man followed me into the communal hallway of my flat while I was living in Brixton and, as I turned, knocked me spark out, chipping one front tooth and, for extra points, killing the root in my other one. The dead tooth slowly went blue over the next couple of years, so ultimately, I sucked the bullet and had my front teeth fixed. They're now expected to do the job of all my teeth: the biting, the tearing, the nibbling. In dining situations, I look like a donkey chewing a Gummi Bear. The rest are now for whatever the opposite of decoration is.

Desecration possibly.

I have suffered for years, decades now, from bruxism. I am a teeth grinder. As I sleep, my jaws grate like miller's wheels, back and forth, slowly destroying my teeth by restless attrition. I can do nothing about it. I'm asleep. As the enamel is ground to powder, there is no protection for the softer inner tooth, so it stains and degrades, and as the process continues the tooth collapses—a cake in the rain—hollowing out, the corners sharpening, becoming brittle. They snap off. I consider myself an optimist because I continue to brush these wizened stubs every day.

I wore a gumshield to bed for many years—it was all could do not to spit into a bucket when I woke in the morning. There was special cleaning product gel you put in the tooth-guard to clean your teeth while you slept. Later, as the pearly whites eroded to shiny flour, a more robust anti-grinding guard was used, and I ground through it like a dog's chew toy.

I've never missed a dental appointment. I brush twice a day. The only reason I don't floss is because I did it once and lopped off a lump of tooth like pared cheese. I spent money on these things when I had it—none of the gels, guards, veneers, or crowns were cheap. I may be slack in other areas, but I've spent a lot of time and money on my teeth, and they still look like an abandoned quarry. It's not my fault. But it's still my smile, it's still the reason I pout like David Sylvian in photos. It's still my shame.

So I'm buying some new teeth this year.

My teeth as a younger man were rather lovely. Regular and clean, slightly goofy in the Cliff Richard manner, but good enough for me to affect a lazy, lopsided smile, something I self-consciously cultivated to show them off. They were the colour of Mini Milks—not the aggressive, Max Headroom smile that's so prevalent now. It's touching the TV presenter, Rylan, famous for the light-sabre gleam of his teeth, had his smile dismantled and rebuilt during a period of depression last year. In a sense the snow-glare grin is the mask Ross, the real Rylan, hides behind. To feel better protected he needed to amplify the wattage. I like Rylan. If you must have TV presenters, he's a fine example.

Do what you have to do, Rylan.

I've no interest in a smile that inhuman. It'll be a big enough wrench for people to see me wandering around with reasonable teeth. I don't want it shining like a low winter sun. I don't want to be a hazard to shipping.

And this won't be the thin end of the wedge. I'm not suddenly going to get into eye-tucks and fillers. I dyed my hair for a few years in my twenties and early thirties, as I started to go grey at the age of 24 and reasoned I had a long time to have grey hair. Because my hair grows like bamboo, I was dying it on a weekly basis. The colour got denser and more unnatural; in the end it looked like Dot Cotton's plum rinse. Under strip-lighting it looked like a head-wound.

The last time I dyed my hair was for my sister's wedding, and I was on crutches for that, having been hospitalised that summer with a broken knee. I caught MRSA while I was on the disgustingly filthy ward, and they put me into a hospice room where they forgot to feed me. I lost three stone over the summer. You should check out my sister's Wedding Album, if only for the scrawny, black-haired scarecrow on sticks at the back of all the photos. And, you know, because she looked like a magical princess on the day, obviously.

I wouldn't mind being a Quentin Crisp in my later years, though I'm already so far past the first flush of youth my entire cistern has packed in. A bit of guy-liner, a splash of drama on the temples, something to excavate the cheekbones wouldn't go amiss. I'd need to drop a couple of stone. Those elderly peacocks are always pared to the bone and arse-free. A big fat blousy one like me would look like Robert Morley's Meredith Merridew in *Theatre of Blood*—doting on twin poodles in a lavender suit. That's a less attractive option.

We all grow old disgracefully now, we're all eternal children—men in their fifties collecting *Star Wars* figures and issuing fatwas on the internet over *Dr Who* casting decisions. There are pensioner punks. I'd be an old New Romantic. Nick Rhodes is a viable role model. I saw him in concert on TV the other day and he was wearing a cravat with a brooch. That takes some doing. He may have to comb his hair *very* carefully these days, but there's nothing wrong with that. He's in his sixties and he's still making pop music. Some might say that's his tragedy, but I think when he carks it, it'll be from an excess of bruising, as he's been pinching himself in disbelief for forty years. It's been a rollercoaster ride of cocaine, supermodels, adulation, screaming Japanese girls, Revlon and polaroid exhibitions. There may even have been a mid-eighties flirtation with food sculpture, once he saw Bowie was doing it. What a life, a life of quiet excess, of tolerable indulgence. He keeps a picture of Stephen "Tin Tin" Duffy in his wallet, just to remind him of how it all could have worked out.

Stephen looks pretty good for his age too, in fact.

St Appollonia of Alexandria, deploying a classic pincer movement

White Smiles of the Rich and Famous

St Apollonia of Alexandria is the patron saint of dentists and those suffering from toothache. As usual with patron saints and the cold-blooded irony we associate with the ancient church, she was tortured by having her teeth smashed or pulled out by pincers. She didn't die from that, she died jumping into a fire, but that's a bit boring, so dentists it is. Punitive tooth extraction has been popular (with the people doing it) throughout history—the phrase "I'd give my eye-tooth for that", allegedly comes from thieves and robbers measuring the weight of the punishment against the crime.

Francisco de Zurbaran's portrait of Saint Apollonia sees her proffering a pair of pliers with a mouth like a cat's bum. Fair enough, of all the martyrs she had least to smile about.

Incidentally, I'd always thought that the "eye" in eye teeth was just a shortening of incisor, but there does appear to have been a wide-spread belief that the eye tooth and the eye were linked in some way. Medieval tooth-pullers (charmingly, and again probably sarcastically, known as "dear hearts") refused to pull incisors for fear of blinding their customers.

George Washington started losing his teeth at 24, and had a single tooth left by the time he was sworn into office as first president of the United States. It was thought for years he had wooden teeth but, in fact, his dentures were furnished with just about anything lying around the house: horse teeth, ivory from both elephants and hippos, shards of metal, even his own, discarded teeth were repurposed and stuck back in again. There's a lot of speculation about George Washington's voice: was it soft or harsh? What kind of accent did he have? But I'm more interested in what his smile looked like. A poorly maintained dry-stone wall, perhaps? The storeroom of a Charity Shop? Chesil beach?

In keeping with what we know of the man, **John Lennon** once decided to gift his housekeeper a freshly removed molar. One of his. He didn't just find it. It wasn't thrown on stage at Shea Stadium. After he died, she put it up for auction and the blood-caked Beatle bit was bought by a Canadian dentist for just shy of $31, 000, slightly less than Isaac Newton's tooth fetched at auction. Which is quite surprising, as nobody wanted a bit of old Isaac when was alive—he died a virgin. The dentist has extracted DNA from the tooth and is looking to clone the former close harmony singer. Like the world doesn't have enough wife-beaters.

Elizabeth the First had famously black, rotten, and smelly teeth. Tooth disease was an indulgence of the rich at that time, as only they could afford sugar or afford the physick to keep them alive past thirty. "I may have the body of a weak and feeble woman, but I have breath that could stun a horse." The Queen is alleged to have said.

Elizabeth is a famously busy ghost, haunting several tenuously linked piles. In one story I recall reading as a child (and which I'm unable to find again) she appeared as a ghost *in negative,* her black teeth white, her pasty face blackened. Imagine that—even as a ghost she still had bad teeth. Doomed to walk her endless, mysterious circuit, drifting silently through the masonry, as ghostly plaque tickles her incorporeal gums. An eternity of toothache. You wouldn't wish it on her dad.

You might.

I think **Elizabeth the Second** had quite nice teeth, but the Queen Mum famously had rows of half-chewed corn niblets. People did then. It was the style of the time. A Hollywood smile would have been very Non-U.

You didn't see a lot of Elizabeth the Second's teeth—most tabloid telephoto shots had her scowling at horse races. But she looks good on a coin. The Royals, generally, have healthy-looking, slightly goofy teeth, after the manner of Monty Python's *Upper-Class Twits*. Prince Andrew and his wife Sarah Ferguson look as though they could chew through girders, so imagine the oral arsenal that princesses Beatrice and Eugenie have inherited, and be thankful that, as far as we know, that's *all* they've inherited.

Van Gogh had terrible teeth, and on arrival in Paris had ten removed in one go. Art scholars claim this is the reason he never smiled in his many self-portraits, but really, can you imagine Van Gogh grinning boyishly in his straw hat and bandage? It's just not his style. It's like thinking Chuck D doesn't smile in photos because he's self-conscious about his gum-line. Van Gogh had a B-Boy attitude. And dentures.

Tom Cruise, now equipped with a grin you can still see when you close your eyes, had famously bad teeth when he was younger. There's a reason his teeth are on full-beam in all his films—he spent a lot of cash on them and needs to get value for money. That's also why he runs in all his films. Oh, you thought they were his *original* legs. So naïve.

The most famous teeth in cinema belong to *Jaws*. Not the shark one. I'm talking about **Richard Kiel's** metal molars in two James Bond adventures. The teeth were apparently very uncomfortable to wear for the actor, and he could only keep them in for very short periods of time before gagging. In the film *Moonraker,* Jaws takes a chunk out of one of the cable car cables. A stunt hawser made of liquorish was used. Cinema is lying to you all the time. It's all tricks and flummery. Richard Kiel is only 5'7"—it's forced perspective.

Of course, the actual most famous teeth in cinematic history belong to **Count Dracula**, who has been biting people in films for a century now and shows no sign of stopping.

Nosferatu was released in 1922, with Max Schreck portraying an emaciated, cadaverous "Count Orlok" in the first (surviving) film to be based on the novel. Bram Stoker's wife took legal action against the film and ordered every print destroyed. Luckily, because the film is strange and beautiful and poetic, she failed. Some prints survived and have delighted people ever since. The year before *Nosferatu* was made, a Hungarian film called *Drakula Halala* ("Dracula's Death") had been released, though it didn't follow the events of the novel, and is now considered a lost film. There is an amazing, existing picture of the actor Paul Askonas portraying Dracula. He looks like Ken Dodd. I really wish that had taken off, instead of Bela Lugosi's drawing-room debonaire, we'd have the Tattyfilarious Terror of Transylvania, traumatised by a tickling stake.

There are debates about how vampire's teeth work all over the internet, but they break down into two main camps: one group believe that a vampire's incisors are just like any other predator's teeth. They use them to bite into a victim's jugular, and just lap at the blood like a pretty little kitten. Others believe that a vampire's teeth are hollow as bird bones and it can suck blood through them, like straws. There are side issues (does the vampire's saliva contain a decoagulant, does he have the power to alter his lung pressure, giving him a more powerful suck?) but it boils down to the bite vs suck camp. And it's the former, isn't it? Obviously. How does one suck through a hollowed-out tooth? Where does the blood go? Into your gums? No, it's the slashing teeth scenario for me.

They do seem to be retractable though. Not sure how that works.

Vampires live for thousands of years. They live in draughty castles with grumbling Medieval plumbing. They spend their time chomping through skin and raw flesh and bone. Yet, they always have great teeth. Even Orlok's rodent over-bite looks clean and strong. This is their most mysterious power. I don't care how Dracula can turn into a pillar of mist, or commune with the other children of the night. I just want to know what his dental regime is. Does Dracula floss? That should be the title of this book—perfect for the Christmas novelty market. "Does Dracula Floss?"

Admit it, that's a stocking filler of a title!

I would no longer make it as a vampire. Beyond my four veneers (the incisors, top row, front) there's a waste-land. The canines are crumbled and stained. Two of the pre-molars missing, the molars jagged hollows, where the tooth has disappeared from the inside out. Only my wisdom teeth remain intact, and wisdom teeth are ut-terly useless. Today my fake front teeth do all the work. They bite, they chew, and if I'm called upon to smile, they stand in for my actual teeth, like a wall of defenders at a penalty shoot-out, the goalie long since crumbled to dust, the goal itself probably moot at this point.

THE BIG BOOK OF BRITISH SMILES

ASK AMERICANS about the "Brits" and a cavalcade of stereotypes canter forth. We are reserved. We are called Nigel. We are sexually repressed. We are quaint. We went to Hogwarts. Tweed is a big deal in our lives, as is talking about the weather and not talking about our feelings. We eat bad food, have bad sex and behave badly at football matches. We have a deliciously dry sense of humour. We're self-deprecating and hate talking about money. We love tea, the monarchy and we know our place, and, above all, we have bad, bad teeth.

None of these things are entirely untrue. Or entirely true. I'm not called Nigel and I never have been. I loathe football and eat well, if unwisely. I'm a prodigious lover versed in all the erotic arts and have no sense of humour at all. I will admit to a fondness for tweed (I have tweed shoes), and I *do* have bad teeth.

However, this makes me a freakish outlier, because the British have better teeth than our American cousins. A study published in *The British Medical Journal* found the average number of missing teeth in British mouths was 6.97 as opposed to the 7.31 in American mouths. Neither figure is great—the UK is not even in the top ten for oral health in Europe—but without America's cultural imperialism—manifest dentistry, if you will—we don't get to hear what the Spanish or Italians think of our teeth, which is probably for the best. We're not popular. No, it's only the US who portrays us as snaggle-toothed upper-class twits. And you haven't got a leg to stand on, Billy Bob.

Say AAAAGH!

You Can't Handle the Tooth

M Y DENTIST, whom I haven't seen for three years because of Covid (and because a non-medical emergency dental appointment now takes six months to get) referred me to a dental clinic. She's a nice woman, and totally backs me on the idea that my awful teeth are beyond my control. I'm like Valmont at the end of *Dangerous Liaisons* every time I'm forced to explain to a dental professional why this awful thing has happened in my mouth.

"It's beyond my control," I simper with a distracted air. "It's beyond my control, and my dentist is willing to back me up on this."

And she does. She points out there's no decay, that the tooth-loss, the staining, the general snaggliness, is all down to the years of attrition. I've been grinding the buggers in my sleep for decades.

I've no idea why. I've been unhappy for large periods of my life, sure, but I've only come to know that retrospectively. In my day we didn't have depression. It was considered perfectly normal for a teenage boy—previously top of every class—to suddenly fail every exam while not talking to anyone for three years. Part of growing up was spending the aftermath of a failed relationship hiding in your parents' attic, drawing comic strips that were never sent to anyone.

I was depressed quite a lot, but I could still get up and feed myself and pull myself together, so I didn't consider myself mad. I'd have quite liked that—wild-eyed in a big shirt, hurling myself onto a coffin, or swigging hemlock in a garret with sheaves of immortal prose scattered about like used Kleenex. There's romance to that, tradition. But this low-level, joyless, trudge through life, meeting each minor inconvenience as an impassable alp, was just how life was. Savourless. Grey. Overcast and disappointingly ugly. At night I'd lie in bed (I had a bed—how bad could things be, really? Pull yourself together) and not sleep until dawn. But when I slept, I ground my teeth, and woke at noon, jaws aching.

But teeth are strong. The damage didn't start to show for a decade, and for years I ground away, developing the bite pressure of a crocodile.

My dentist referred me to a specialist clinic who rang me with indecent haste, offering an appointment for the very next day. My dental records make delicious reading for people who profit from tarting up gums.

The new clinic is only about twenty minutes away, so I walked there. It rained, of course, and I had no umbrella, despite living in a country where it rains every day. The sign on the door said, "Masks Must Be Worn", so I went inside, mask on, wiping down my rain-fogged glasses. When the steam cleared, I found that no one was wearing a mask, so I took mine off and sat in the waiting room. It's a clean room. Some of the dentists I attended in London mirrored the horrors of my mouth: they were like desecrated churches, lumps of stucco gouged from the wall, all dead plants and dust. This one has semi-circle of functional grey chairs, a faux hardwood floor, an aspidistra in a terracotta pot and cabinet full of toothbrushes and mouthwash. The cabinet's locked, which is a nice touch. There are two receptionists chatting away behind a plastic screen. There are dull prints of Irish coastal villages on the wall.

I get the call, and I'm met, halfway up the stairs, by the Dentist who looks momentarily as if he wants to shake my hand, but we hesitate and the moment is gone. He looks like a tall Reece Shearsmith, without the rage. And why would he be raging? He's about to relieve me of a lot of money. As he makes his initial investigation into the blasted heath of my mouth, I see the pound signs dancing in his eyes. Am I mistaken? Does the mask start to colour slightly as he salivates at the prospect? Judging by the faraway cast in his eye he's already waving his kids off to university.

He has me stand against a wall and takes a series of mug-shot-style photos: left profile, right profile, straight ahead but, crucially, smiling, widely. This is my idea of a nightmare. I am deeply ashamed of my teeth. People have mocked me for years for pouting in photos. I'm a fifty-year-old man posing like Derek Zoolander in the presence of a paparazzi flashbulb. It looks ridiculous, of course. But the alternative is flashing these tarnished splinters, the negative space, the pulped gums, the tea-stained gravel at the cold eye of the camera's lens. I'd rather you thought I was a twat than an ogre, though that's a personal choice. And here I am doing it. Teeth bared. My horrible naked teeth.

Next, I'm in the chair for X rays, and the Dentist starts filling my mouth with what appear to be full-size oars. Every time they set up the X Ray, he and the Nurse run out of the room like the cowards they are, leaving me alone in the blast zone. During one intrusive jab the tip of my incisor snaps off, audibly. We look at each other. "Was that a bit of plastic?" he says. I locate the foreign object, fish it out of my mouth and having no better idea what to do with it, hand it to him. It is a small shard of bone.

"Ah, no." he says. I don't know what he did with the tooth, but he didn't attempt to stick it back on.

It's like the Ludovico Technique, as I lie back, my eyes shining, and he fills my mouth with what can only be furniture. He tells me that the tooth erosion means that my jaw has misaligned and attempts to snap it back into place AND IT GOES BACK INTO PLACE. My head is now a different shape. Does it hurt? Only initially. Only when I don't know it's coming.

He shows me the photos he's taken of my teeth.

My God.

They're illuminated on a lightboard, and the detail is extraordinary. My teeth are disgusting. I knew it was bad, but I didn't know it was this bad, because nothing in nature could be *this* bad. There's a quality of marine life: a contaminated coral reef, or the stunted, long vacated shells of withered bivalves, a spilt treasure trove of encrusted doubloons, corroded currency, polluted pearls and cloudy, lightless gemstones. Equally, as it's on a lightbox and super colour-saturated, it looks like a gruesome mixed grill in a greasy spoon: baked beans, offal, curling buttered bread. Fried mushrooms, gleaming under a bare bulb.

I'm so upset I can barely look at it, but he seems very pleased, pointing out the various empty areas, the hollows, the ruts, like he was giving a lecture on the South Downs: the peaks and promontories, abandoned follies, areas of outstanding natural ugliness. I wonder if I can get the National Trust to pay for this.

After an hour and shelling out the best part of two hundred pounds for this humiliation, I stagger home, reeling from the trauma. I wake up in a cold sweat that night, haunted by my own leopard print smile, black on yellow like an aged banana.

A couple of weeks later I receive a document in the post, a lengthy report detailing the timeline for any work done: the order of work (all the extractions—seven of them—first), recovery time, options for replacements, from implants to dentures. And of course, the cost. The report was illustrated with a couple of the glorious photos the Dentist had taken of my teeth, which basically said "I know this is a lot of money but come on mate— look at the state of your gnashers." It was an excellent strategy. The teeth will cost a lot of money. They will be, in fact, the most expensive thing I've ever bought, and I once put (half) a deposit on a flat in London. (It wasn't a very nice flat and I was mugged in our shared hallway, but even so . . .)

I currently have some money. And my teeth are a source of shame to me. More than that, they physically hurt me. The left upper tooth, a hollow with a sharp rim, often aches. The teeth themselves gouge into my cheeks and tongue at intervals. No, I can't carry on with these teeth. I want to make an investment in a smile that will outlive me.

My friend Shauna tells me she's never noticed my teeth, that I'm just paranoid about them, like she is about her fat ankles (she doesn't have fat ankles). But I don't believe her, because the first thing I do when I meet someone is sneakily look at their teeth, judging and appraising them, looking for discolouration and decay, and Shauna has never once glanced at the width of my ankles. Teeth tell you everything about a person—even after you're dead they can tell people what your diet was like. While you're alive, teeth like mine tell people you sleep nightly under a piss-soaked newspaper and the stars.

Check Out my Gravel Pit

COUPLE OF WEEKS later I received a voice message on my phone asking me what I wanted to do. From the Dentist, not generally. I phoned and they initially thought I was someone else, then got confused about what I was asking, could find no sign of me on their system, and finally told me the Dentist wasn't there, and could he ring me in four days' time. Today is four days later and he hasn't rung me, I've rung him, and the switchboard went straight to voicemail. So, I left a message asking him to phone me and he hasn't. Bodes well for the single greatest expenditure of my life. It's like I'm attempting to arrange my own costly and protracted torture, and no one will do it. You'd think they'd be queuing up.

Reassuringly, the report starts with "I am pleased to report no adverse findings on routine oral cancer screening." That's a very positive start, though I have no recollection of him doing or saying he was going to do an oral cancer screening. But really, there was a lot going on and it was intense. He might very well have snuck that in there. So, thanks. A positive start. It drops off pretty quickly.

The first part of the report is called "Stabilisation."

The treatment plan contains: an abscess, requiring an extraction or root canal. Two unrestorable broken teeth requiring extraction. A severely worn tooth. Another severely worn tooth. Three more worn teeth. A failing crown tooth requiring extraction. Old crowns on four teeth, the edges of which are failing. Nine more severely worn teeth.

He wants to extract seven of my teeth and for me to pay him nearly a £1000 to do so. I'll be a grand in the hole to look worse. All sunken cheeks and wobbling jowls. I'm hoping the pain and inconvenience will be a great way of losing weight. If it hurts to eat, and everything tastes like a wound anyway, you'd think it'd be boon to slimming. But booze is a liquid. Ice cream melts. You can put a cheeseburger in a blender. Gluttony, like nature, finds a way.

The Dentist rang back the next day, and we arranged my first appointment and, as usual when I'm talking to people I don't know, I attempted to make him like me. It's getting worse. When I was young, I suspected everyone hated me and was a study of icy indifference. People thought I was arrogant and distant, and I was never more attractive and popular. Now I'm middle-aged and as erotic as hairy porridge, which I also strongly resemble, I see no reason why people *shouldn't* like me. I'm harmless. So, I smile (without showing my teeth). I make eye contact. I tell jokes.

My friend Jackie has suggested I might be suffering from a neurological condition called *Witzelsucht*, characterised by a tendency to make puns and tell inappropriate jokes. It makes you unable to read sarcasm, which is a bit of a stretch. A less common symptom is hypersexuality. The patient believes their behaviour to be normal and is therefore unresponsive to other's reactions.

Now.

That's clearly quite insulting. I am, after all, merely trying to get people to like me. I'm trying to make you laugh. I'm not suffering from a frontal lobe injury. Though it does prove that funny men *really* are sexy, just inappropriately. I don't believe I'm suffering from a neurological condition unless it's one called "wit". But I sometimes overdo it, and that's what I was doing with my dentist on the phone while he was clearly doing a business transaction and suffering along with my jokes until he can close the sale. First thing they teach you in dentistry: always be closing.

I start in mid-January. I thought it best to get Christmas out of the way. I'm not sure why. My initial appointment will include the seven extractions.

John: "How long will that take?"

Dentist: "About an hour."

John: "An hour? For seven teeth? That's some going. How are you going to get them out anyway? Most of them are just little bits."

Dentist: "You think I'm going use pliers, don't you?"

John: "Or a bit of string and a door."

Dentist: I use a precision tool to delicately cut the tooth's ligament from the jawbone. It's quite simple."

John: "That's quite a bedside manner. That almost sounds pleasant. How about sedation?"

Dentist: "Do you want sedation? We could do that."

John: "What do other people do?"

Dentist: "Only about a quarter of them have sedation."

John: "Yeah, alright. I won't bother. I'm pretty good with dentists. Despite the evidence."

Dentist: "We can have some on standby if you change your mind."

John: "With a mouthful of blood and cotton wool. I don't need a safety word—I need a safety gesture. A vigorous one!"

Dentist: "Ha ha"

On it goes, until I agree to pay him a vast sum of money to remove bits of my head. I won't be laughing then. His practice is on the first floor. I wonder how many people, faint and enfeebled from blood loss, fall down the stairs and smash their heads on the wood laminate flooring? I hope I'm not the first to christen it.

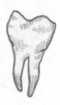

First Appointment, Last Rites

I BECAME TERRIFIED of the Dentist's stairs. For weeks I worried about his practice being on the first floor, and had visions of staggering from his chair and, hare-eyed, spitting blood and enamel, immediately falling down his stairs. I'd remembered them as wide, white marble, with golden stair-rods, like Liberace's fire escape. In fact, they're narrow, carpeted, with sturdy banisters on both sides. They're utterly safe. I'd completely misremembered them.

I've had my teeth, like The Archies' *Sugar Sugar*, stuck in my head for a very long time. We've been through good times and bad, but they've always been there for me, except when bits were falling off, cracking, discolouring and throbbing. But today seven of these life-long bad tenants are being evicted. I could name them: Achey, Splintery, Barely-Therey, Chippy, Stainy, Ghastly and

Grizzled-Battle-Scarred-Castle-Collapsing-Into-The-Seay. But I won't. I'm not sentimental.

Seven's a lot. But you have thirty-two teeth, and if you remove seven you still have twenty-five and that's plenty, right? Right?

I'm nervous. The waiting room is empty but for a red-faced bald man angrily thumbing at his phone. The receptionists seem cross, but I don't know why. This must be a gift of a job. No one is here, no one is ringing in, they're just chatting and staring at screens. That's my downtime. There's probably a bit more to it.

There's a TV on the wall over my head so I don't have to see it. It's showing *The Apprentice*. Why does every medical facility in the world have a plasma screen pouring shit into the waiting room? I'm paying a lot of money for this bespoke torture, but the customer experience is practically identical to my lengthy waits in the Dole Office from a couple of years ago: the same angry women behind protective glass, the same angry men stabbing at their I-phones, the same babbling bullshit from the TV, except now there's a drill accompanying Lord Sugar's piss-weak scripted one-liners. God, I hate him.

My foot's going to sleep. Maybe I could focus on that while they're ripping my face to pieces. Will they tear the corner of my mouth this time? Will bits of other teeth chip off as collateral damage? I've had some cowboys up in my grill in the past.

The bald man has gone. I'm alone in the waiting room, scratching into my notebook, when the dentist appears, beaming beneath his mask. It's time to make my appointment with the Dentist's chair.

Midway through the treatment, my mouth numbed in four separate directions—like wearing a beard of ice— the Dentist starts to chat to me about my film career. His first cousin has directed films for the festival circuit. He gives me the name, but I don't know it. He then admits he's never seen any of them. I attempt to describe my latest film, but my mouth is compromised in complicated ways. My bottom lip is rubbery, like a split inner-tube. I feel my mouth falling into a full Cumberland sausage sulk. Plosives are impossible. I'm a bad ventriloquist and dummy combined.

Things I find out about myself in the Mastermind chair. I am surprisingly resistant to anaesthetic. "It happens," says the Dentist, mysteriously, and I think he suspects me of being a long-term heroin user. I find out I have "complicated roots". The first tooth is out almost immediately, before I think he's seriously engaged with it, and I think "This is brilliant—we'll be out well under the scheduled 45 minutes". But the next tooth is IN there—

the sword in the stone of my gums. It's not shifting at all. A drill is produced, vibrating through my skull and causing strange heart palpitations. Great, I think, I'm going to have a heart attack in the dentist's chair. That's what people do now—dying in your fifties is fashionable. I flinch and he stops.

"Are you okay? Are you having pain?"

I have neither the verbal equipment or mime skills to indicate I'm about to have a heart attack, but the sensation abruptly stops when the drill isn't fracking my skeleton, and he returns to snipping the roots off my complex tooth.

We stop proceedings to take an Xray of my jaw to make sure all the bits are out—my teeth have roots like a mighty oak, and I note the irony that my feeble, buttermilk teeth are incredibly resilient beneath the gum-line. The roots on this tooth appear to be heart-shaped, and I think of the mandrake plant, and what a boon to a witches' cauldron a heart-shaped tooth root might be. Anyway, it's out. Two down, five to go.

I should say I'm wearing sunglasses throughout this ordeal. Bono-style wraparounds. They're provided—I didn't bring them from home. They're so I can stare into the halo of white lights above me. When I close my eyes, I can still see the lights, like pomegranate seeds spilled on velvet, red on black, as the drill pushes in again. It's hard work.

I wonder what it must be like to be a dentist. To wake up in the morning with the certain knowledge that at an agreed time you will be pulling teeth out of someone's head. Get up, shower, bit of toast. Drive to the office. Chat to the receptionist, do some admin. Then drilling holes in people, dragging teeth out of them, snapping the roots, numbing their outraged gums. Spot of lunch. Sandwiches in a Tupperware box. Gloves still on.

Must be odd.

At one point the Dentist can't work his drill ("It's never done that before"). At another a wheel falls off his trolley. It's like Norman Wisdom starring in *Marathon Man*. At some other time—I can no longer tell the precise order of events—someone else is in the room with us. I'm lying there, gob wide-open in my Peters and Lee specs, staring into a halogen lamp with a petrified jaw. I'm not aware of anything, barring the blazing white and an occasional gloved hand dropping into the dead mouth I've dissociated from. The lower part of my head is someone else's playground, like a paddling pool or an odds 'n' sods drawer for people to rifle through, looking for bits of string or bayonet lightbulbs.

I listen to the radio. It's tuned to a station that pretends no music has been made in the last 25 years: INXS' *The Devil Inside*, George Harrison's *Got My Mind Set on You*, Coldplay's *Clocks* (inevitably) and Billy Joel's *We Didn't Start the Fire*. *Clocks* soundtracks a particularly vigorous bit of digging, my teeth like trenchant potatoes, and one accompanied by what the Dentist repeatedly calls "sound effects" i.e., the audible cracking of my teeth. It doesn't exactly hurt but I can feel the resistance, deep in my jaw and neck, hear the crack of my splintering enamel, feel the drill deep into my roots, into the meat of me.

The last two teeth are, of course, the worst. We've been at it for well over an hour and my anaesthetic is beginning to wear off, so I'm getting more and more injections. The last two teeth require stitches and I'm treated to the uniquely peculiar sensation of someone pushing a needle and thread through my naked, empty gums. They say you should experience everything once, but there have been quite a few events over the last hour and a half (forty-five minutes, my arse) I don't feel were an ornament to my life experience. This was not swimming with dolphins.

And it's over. There was a lot of last-minute action, a final skirmish, scrabbling to get over the top . . . and it's done. The dental assistant, who has not said a single word throughout, swabs my mouth and chin, and I realise I'm probably covered in blood. Of course, I am—I've been swallowing copper juice for an hour, some of it must have leaked out. Luckily, I'm wearing shades and a pinny.

I sit up and plump my hair (still cool) and ditch the shades for my proper glasses. I feel like I might be in mild shock. I have the hare-eyed expression of a man who has been mugged by a ghost and is now obliged to tell people about it. The Dentist, flushed, mask still on, congratulates me on doing so well. He has been calling me a "good man" throughout, pleased I decided not to have a heart attack during the ordeal, sparing him additional paperwork. He tells me to alternate paracetamol and ibuprofen, not to eat "difficult food" (ok), not drink "piping hot drinks" and swill my mouth out with salty water, but not until tomorrow. He asks me if I smoke and looks doubtful when I say no—he's seen my teeth. They make me look as if I do *everything*.

And that's it. I bowl out the door, easily negotiate the stairs and meet the receptionist, only this time I can't talk. This seems to make her like me more. I pay her an enormous amount of money and make an appointment for two root canals in a months' time. I use their toilet and the light goes off twice while I'm pissing. Seems to be the way it's going.

I head outside. It's dark now but Susan is in the car waiting to take me home. Numbed and speechless, a reddening paper towel to my lips, I let her.

I posted on Facebook that I'd had seven teeth removed. Why? Why do I post anything on Facebook ever? Is it because I never go out and therefore never see anybody? And now these are my only conversations, my social interactions—"Hello! I'm still here. I'm still bright and funny. I still have opinions."

When I post something innocuous like "I'm watching—insert name of TV program or film—and I really like it", I'm just expressing an opinion. It doesn't require a rebuttal.

But that's what you get, every time, and always the first reply: "Hello, I like a thing." "No, the thing you like is shit." "Okay. Do you want me to tell you I'm wrong? Is that it? That another, cleverer man made me see the error of my ways in a concise manner? I thought I liked something, but must have been wrong, because this cool customer didn't. Sorry."

Worse still, there are people saying, "I thought I hated it but, based on your assessment, I will watch the rest of the series." NO! please don't. Trust your instincts. Not everything is for everyone. You might hate it. To quote Spandau Ballet, once again, "I don't need this pressure on."

Another dislike—so, so many—is, when posting a song I like, someone immediately posts another song and says, "Have you heard *this* song though?" the implication being they've now trumped my song with a better one. Maybe I'm being paranoid. I'm sure that does happen with shut-ins, spooked by the peculiar motivations of alien minds— what do they really mean by "have you heard this?" Of course I've heard it. I've heard *everything* I could ever want to hear. How dare you try opening exciting new vistas for me. I am a lone traveller kayaking up my own narrow fundament, listening to the same ten albums in strict rotation. I have rendered all music a thick, gelatinous reduction, now I'm spooning it into my ears. Thank you, no.

(Only today, I discovered I really like Cleaners from Venus from a friends mix-CD, and I'm listening to my copy of Mellow's *Perfect Colors* which I've owned for three years and never listened to. Both are delightful.)

So, I'm mad and freakish and institutionalised and usually wrong. That much has been established. But I'm not wrong about this: if I post that I've had seven teeth removed in a single sitting, what I'm looking for is sympathy and good wishes. And, half the time, that's what I got. Not everyone is evil.

But what I also got was also dire warning that I was *definitely* going to get the innocuous sounding "dry socket", and the subsequent pain was "the most excruciating pain" ever experienced. This is the day *after* the surgery, not the day before when I could have talked to the dentist about it. No, this is my recovery time so there's nothing to be done but take the feeble precautions the Dentist has offered: rinse with salt water, don't drink hot beverages, be careful about what you eat. That's it. Job's comforters aren't in it.

A dry socket occurs when the scab over the wound falls away and the ragged hole in your gum becomes infected. I told my correspondents that I was gurgling away with salt water. "That won't save you—I rinsed like Billy O and still got it. Agony. Worse than childbirth." When a woman tells you her pain was worse than childbirth, you *have* to listen. That is the upper metric of ladypain, that's the bomb they drop when you're complaining about whatever feeble ache you're suffering with. Legless veterans describing land-mine encounters are summarily dismissed by young mothers still waiting for their stitches to melt. Men have nothing. And so, there was no escaping it. It was a done deal. An added feature of the surgery was searing, inevitable pain the dentist hadn't bothered to mention.

I looked it up. A "dry socket" affects between 2 and 5% of people who have teeth removed. It's more prevalent in smokers and women on birth control. It's most likely to happen in the first 48 hours.

Four days after the surgery my gums are tender in the morning, but I'm comfortably managing the pain with paracetamol. I'm no longer spitting blood. I'm eating soup and brushing the remaining teeth with a baby's toothbrush that Susan bought me. I'm not out of the woods yet—it can still happen up to a week later. But I'm being cautious. And I'm not yet in agony. Sorry to disappoint you, ghouls.

After a week my gums are febrile and tender, but my tongue is getting braver around them, pushing into the cavities where my teeth used to be. It's becoming a recognisable landscape. I'm starting to map it. I can feel the thread of my stitches, lower right, like a shoelace knotted on top of the soft, pink ballet slipper of my gum. The geography of your mouth is always enormous, your tongue is a sandworm nosing through the "Dune" planet, discovering ghostly canyons, carved out caves, and now a soft, coppery desert. Nevertheless, I'm getting used to it, which is a fool's errand as, soon as my gums are healed,

I'm due a root canal which will tunnel into them all over again, hacking up divots of serrated gum flesh.

I'd hoped the gums would be less tender after a few days and, in fact, thought I'd got away with it. The day after the operation I felt almost no pain. It was like a magic trick. I was stunned and spent the day wide-eyed and grinning (the front teeth are still on—I can grin in a limited way). It was like a lottery win. Susan too was incredibly relieved. I was exceptionally careful, and ate nothing but a bowl of cold soup, being careful to disallow my inquisitive tongue to stray into these new channels and ruts, my mouth a recently ploughed field.

I remained careful throughout the following week, anxious to avoid the searing pain promised me by well-wishers. Historically, I'm a good healer, which is not a nice thing to have to find out about yourself and, at the back of my mind, I was convinced the mincemeat of my gums would have hardened by the weekend. They hadn't and a week on the gums are still tender and raw. I can't help but be disappointed.

My diet is dull. I start the day with the first of several brine rinses. Then I heat up a tin of soup and allow it to go cold, so I can spoon it into the tortured meat of my mouth. I drink smoothies and cold coffee and tea throughout the day. Dinner is either scrambled eggs, an omelette or mashed Shepherd's Pie, swimming in gravy so it too becomes like a thick soup. I made the mistake, early in the process of attempting a breaded fishcake in a cheese sauce. It was delicious, but my gums were throbbing and itchy for the next two days. I've entered a world of mush. A banana was too acid for my baby mouth, even crushed with a fork. I've had no bread, no meat that wasn't minced, no cheese that wasn't melted and then congealed as it cooled again. I miss garlic. I miss strong cheese. I miss crunch. I'm living off tepid slop. I can't properly eat an apple. And I expect this will be my life for the next four or five months. Our birthdays and Valentine's Day are contained within that timeframe, the occasions we're most likely to celebrate with a slap-up feed. Susan could eat, of course. And I could sit there with a celeriac fondant cooling in front of me as she gorges. She might as well, there's no reason for her to suffer. But she won't. She's too kind. She won't be able to enjoy her food with me looking on with the sad, defeated eyes of a dog begging scraps at the table.

The next step is a root-canal, slated for the week before Valentine's Day. I'm giddy with the romance of it all.

MORE ROOT CANALS
THAN VENICE

Second Appointment

I'M PROMISED three root canals in total. That's a boring slog. My appointment was at three but it's now a quarter past and I'm still in the waiting room. I wanted to go to a cash machine and check my balance. I'd been paid for some work, and I wanted to gloat at my miser's horde before I had to spend it all on teeth. There were two cash-points proximate to the dentist, one on the way there and one slightly past it, so I went to the first one and there were two people queuing. This never happens. I've never seen anyone queuing at this bank before. I'm not a very patient man. It's a personal failing, but I don't like to wait. I don't like to hang about, doing nothing. I thought, I have the time, I'll go to the *other* cash machine. I stroll past the dentist and on to the next hole-in-the-wall which is, I now discover, quite a bit further than I'd realised and, when I get there, there are two people queuing at it. What's going on? Why this sudden rush on ATMs? I thought we were a post-cash society. Everywhere you go you see young people paying for their flat whites with their phones. Who are these old farts, clinging to the certainties of the Queen's portrait? And why now, when I just want to stare longingly at the money in my account before the dentist spirits it away. I haven't the time to queue, so I race back to the dentist, arriving a minute after three and expecting a bollocking from the receptionist, only to sit, pink and gently perspiring, for a further fifteen minutes until the dentist appears, beaming beneath his mask.

An aside: I agree to meet a friend in town the next day, at the same time, and make a special note to see if the cash machines were as densely crowded when I didn't need to use them. Of course, no one was at either machine, confirming my theory that the universe hates me and cleverly only displays this enmity in tiny, petty ways that make me sound like a lunatic when I complain about them. It's a slow game of attrition, and grinds exceeding small. It's working too.

I don't get three root canals, just the one today. It is a complex one. It's also the most expensive of the three— my root canals are individually priced in the dentist's plan.

Last time I was in the Dentist's chair, I died. On my arse. My jokes went for nothing, twice—as they used to say in *Vaudeville*. This time I'm *killing* the room. Everything I say gets a laugh and later, when my mouth is incapacitated by rubber-gloved thumbs, my mimes are still wrecking the joint. I'm on fire. I'm not sure what has caused this sea-change, but I'm pathetically grateful for it. It's important to me, as the film I just directed is not going well in the edit and has involved several bruising encounters with my producers where my dialogue has been called into question. I think this is projection mainly— I'm a middle-aged man writing dialogue for people in their twenties. The producers don't think I'm convincing. I contend that people can dredge up startlingly archaic phrases and ideas at times of crisis. But the producers would prefer their young people to be urban and generic. This is what I'm thinking about as the Dentist prepares me for two hours of oral excavation.

My wounds have healed very well. I assumed they would—experience has taught me to heal efficiently. And to be careful descending the stairs. The Dentist looks very pleased with his handiwork, though really the healing was all mine.

He erects a small Navvy's tent on my face, a blue rubber pagoda pegged into my mouth with smooth plastic clips. I'm pleased he's not using this as an excuse to have a crafty wheeze on a tight woodbine or sip weak tea from a battered tin mug. It reminds me of two things: years ago, I had surgery that required the running of a Hickman line directly into my heart. They put a papery blue cloth over my face throughout, because the local anaesthetic was not hiding the horror of masked men pushing pointy objects into my actual heart. Apparently, I'm tougher than the average vampire. It was a distressing, alienating experience. I couldn't quite feel what was going on, but I was very aware of a vigorous tugging at the core of me, the knock-on of activity echoing through my body. I could also hear surgeon chat which you don't want to hear.

The other thought my situation triggers is the eating of an ortolan. I've never eaten an ortolan—a small bird related to the finch—but it is considered a delicacy in France, where it is eaten plucked but otherwise whole, cooked in cognac, the head bitten off and discarded by the diner. Everything else, bones, skin, offal, is consumed. The tradition holds that it should be eaten beneath a cloth, as though you were reading a book by torchlight under the covers. This is to help you better appreciate the subtle flavour of the cooked bird, but there are those who say it is to hide the cruelty of the ortolan's despatching from the eyes of God. I mean this is France. It's hard to call this crueller than the manufacture of goose liver pate, but legends gonna legend.

I was lying back with my mouth open with a blue rubber tepee being erected on my chin. Unusual. The Bono sunglasses were back on, the standard "sharp scratch" was introduced into my gums and the roof of my mouth. I could see nothing that was going on. I stared up into the light, a peculiar luminous iris staring back at me, the eye of Sauron staring you out, as you submit to oral attack. It's a long process and I don't feel particularly involved. Like all surgery, it's just stuff happening to your body. Some ill-defined, numb, abstracted part of me. I just let him get on with it.

I drift. Eyes closed. The fiddly, exploratory bits are fine. When he's gouging and cleaning, that's fine too. But the drill is awful. I've always been proud of my stoicism in the Dentist's chair. I sit there and take it. I soak it up, like the doughty peasant I am. I'm canon-fodder. That's my lot in life. The difference being I'm paying for the cannonball that will take my head off.

The drill is vibrating through me, echoing through my skeleton. It shivers through the meat of me, marbling my fat and making me feel unwell. I attempt to practice mindfulness, to close my eyes and drift off, but I'm experiencing sudden (mild) arrhythmia and I'm slightly worried I'm going to expire in the Dentist's chair, too shy to say anything. I always knew this was how I was going to die: an easily preventable scenario where I was too polite to point out my life-threatening peril. It's fine. Don't worry about it. Nothing to see. Aaaaaaaagh. It's the ideal death for the sort of Englishman I am: quiet, diffident, self-effacing, unfussy and not really English. I know my friends will easily recognise me from that description.

It goes on and on. I've had my mouth open for what seems like days but is probably just an hour. The drilling has stopped and so have my sudden, panicky lurches that give the Dentist pause.

"You okay?"

A weak thumbs up, and he returns to the coal face. I've regulated my saliva, which is tidal, pooling and draining, and I'm managing an exploratory wipe of my dry teeth with the wrung-out leather of my tongue. I have always lived like this. There was never a before time, never a point in my life where a masked man wasn't drifting though the chasms of my mouth. At one point my mouth fills with a nasty bitter taste, but I can't tell whether this is some chemical element he's brought in to sluice my new hollows, or whether this is some disgusting poison my infected tooth has concocted and stashed in an area the Dentist previously called the "Chasm of Infection" on the X-ray, a lagoon of bile secreted in my swollen gum. I have a feeling that I've just struck oil. Thar she blows. It's a gusher.

And then it's over. There is a smooth, pearly white cap over my tooth. There's no pain. And later, when I get home, there's no pain. In the morning, I wake and there's no pain. I'm so impressed. How can anyone stab you in the gums for two hours and there's no tenderness at all? I'm paying a lot for these creeping renovations but it's clearly a solid job.

APPOINTMENT 3

More Roots than Sherwood Forest

HE TEACHERS are out on strike today as I walk to the dentist. They're waving flags about and wearing gilets, as the passing cars beep their solidarity. You go, girl. Funny, I think, every one of those teachers is a blonde woman, as I plod towards the inevitable hollowing of my head.

I'm nervous in the normal manner. The normal manner meaning I talk a lot in a pathetic attempt to make the Dentist like me. Is this learned behaviour? A hangover from school, when I would attempt to make the bullies laugh to deter them from punching me in the face. It generally worked then, but there's a disconnect in this situation—I'm literally paying this man to hurt me. I think of the villain Scorpio, brilliantly played by Andrew Robinson, in the film *Dirty Harry*. As part of his attempt to frame Harry he pays a man to beat him up, giggling perversely with each sickening crunch of knuckle on nose.

I am Scorpio, giggling in the Dentist's chair as he flays my naked gums while, as usual, Michael Hutchence sings about a *Suicide Blonde*. I've not heard so much *INXS* since the late 80s, but every time I'm strapped into the big, black chair they appear, lending further associative terror. I shall forever think of Michael's corkscrew curls as the agony flashes hot and red.

I'm having two root canals today. They are nothing. Next to the trauma of the things that have already happened in my head, a couple of innocuous deep dives into my gums are pretty vanilla. I lie back and think of Martin Amis. It's not that sexy.

I'd been reading *Experience*, Amis's marvellous book about the murder of his cousin, Lucy Partington, at the hands of West Country troglodyte Fred West, about the death of his father, comic novelist and booze enthusiast Kingsley. And about his teeth. Amis famously got a million-pound advance for his novel *The Information* and spent most of it on his blighted choppers. Amis is a dazzling writer and, that rarity, a genuinely funny one, and is very funny on his teeth. But what he mainly writes about is the pain of owning corroded, precarious, untrustworthy teeth. They trouble him with agonies. They are a constant presence, niggling away, the pain searing or dull, reverberating, echoing though the jaw, to a spot behind the eye. They are as unceasing as the devils tormenting St Anthony. Which is a reference he wouldn't use. His teeth pick on him. He's bullied by the ugly little brutes.

I never had that.

My teeth got worse. They melted away. Great craters appeared in the molars, the tips sharpening, my incisors turning to isabelline sickles. The bottom teeth developed fat, hollow ruts, tannin-stained trenches. It was a mess in there, like an abandoned dugout.

But they were never that painful. A touch sensitive at times. I swerved ice cream after a while. But I got away with it. Or maybe my sensitivity to pain became more robust. Once you've broken a knee, there's not much more pain can show you. It's played its trump card.

This is not a challenge. I'm not challenging the fates here. I'm touching wood. I'm good for pain, thanks very much. I've had plenty.

An hour and a half later I descend the stairs into the Dentist's waiting room, lips inflated to somewhere between Michelle Pfeiffer and Donald Duck. I go to make the next two (two!) appointments with the receptionist, and she gives me a card with the dates on.

"OK, that's you," she says, which is Northern Irish for "Go away now, please."

"Don' I hab to bay?"

"There's nothing here, love." She peers at the computer. "No."

"Thass odd. I always baid before."

"Maybe you'll need to pay next time."

"OK." Confused, I head to the door.

Out in the street the teachers are still there waving their flags. They've set up a little table with flasks on it. Cars are tooting their horns, but it doesn't take much for the Northern Irish to toot on their horns. They love it, especially if they've just seen me step onto a zebra-crossing. I stroll past them, wondering if I should say "beep beep" like the Road Runner as I pass. What a delightful little joke. They'd love me. But I don't do it as I'm self-conscious about my swollen face. So, I keep my head down.

As I get to the junction near my house, I feel my phone vibrating in my pocket. Unknown number. I know exactly who it is.

"Hello?"

"Mr Higgins? Sorry were you driving?"

"No, I was walking."

"WALKING?" she says, involuntarily. In Northern Ireland this is not done without the excuse of a dog. It transpires that I do, in fact, have to pay. She quotes the figure, and my eyes start to water. I turn back and pass the picket line I passed only ten minutes before. A couple of eyes meet mine.

The reception area has been left unattended. I stand at the desk, my debit card in my hand, trying to project my sighs past the glass. The receptionist appears from the office with a steaming mug of tea in her hand.

"You're a quick walker!"

I pay the astronomical sum, and she suggests "I bet you wish you'd kept walking".

I leave, poor.

Outside, the picket line is experiencing a lull in traffic and, as I approach, a couple of them eye me warily, as I'm walking past them for the third time in twenty minutes. Now is the time for a spirited Mr Toad "Poop Poop", but my nerve goes, and I shuffle past like the pervert they think I am. Besides, they're teachers—I don't trust them to get the reference. I'm reminded of Calvino's short story "The Naked Breast" where Mr Palomar, walking on a beach, passes a topless woman sunbathing. So anxious is he to put her at ease, he assays a series of different approaches, back and forth: cautious, respectful, unanimous, indifferent, until the flustered woman gathers up her clothes and leaves. That's what they think this is: some delinquent grey-haired gawper getting an eyeful of a host of golden educators blooming all over the pavement.

I keep my head down. If they could see my involuntary "kissy" face, I don't think it would help my case.

FOURTH APPOINTMENT

No Veneer in 'Ere

THIS WAS THE ONE I was dreading. I've had a lot of teeth out—you could plant a sword wielding skeleton army to bash up the Argonauts with my discarded molars. My gums have been number than Ranulph Fiennes's fingertips for weeks now. But the Dentist—a hairy forearmed bruiser, more like a blacksmith than any medical professional I've ever met—wants to pull the caps off my front teeth "to see what's under there". I don't share his curiosity. I'd leave well enough alone. There be dragons. What's with this pioneering spirit anyway. "I'd like to pull off your front tooth." "Why?" "BECAUSE IT'S THERE."

My front four teeth are capped. They're capped because of the mugger who punched me so hard in the mouth he killed the nerve in one front tooth and snapped the other. So, I had those teeth capped and, since the removal of my molars, they've been doing all the work for me: chewing, biting, smiling. Representing.

There's a psychological aspect as well. You don't really see the back teeth. You don't see mine at any rate—I'm not a big laugher. The front ones are the heavy lifters. And he's snapping them out today, to better see the wriggling morbidities beneath. But I've agreed to this. And I'll be paying for it too.

After an hour I lose track of what's going on. I'm not getting my proper new teeth today. I'm getting transient, place-keeper teeth. He's putting these in, then at my next appointment—which he imagines will take all afternoon—he'll build up my bottom front teeth. Then, later, he'll remove these temporary efforts and put in the proper ones. Okay. Sounds a bit . . . counter intuitive. But what the hell? It's only vast amounts of my money I'd otherwise waste on memories and experiences.

After that first hour—and the session eventually takes about two and a half, which is long time to lie on your back with your mouth open—I start to refocus my thoughts. He's stripping the teeth down with a combination of a drill and a strong water jet and listing the teeth as he goes, working right to left. But my attention is elsewhere. I'm concentrating, hard, on not drowning. A lot of water is flooding into my mouth, washing away the debris from my denuded pegs and it has nowhere to go but down my throat. I manage to sluice some into waiting lagoons in my cheeks, or the foot-well beneath my tongue, and I take strategic gasps whenever he moves away. I'm not being melodramatic when I say it's exactly like being waterboarded. Well, I am, but I definitely would have talked, had I not had a gob-full of fluid, fingers and drills. Eventually I did choke and had to do my safety gesture—a frantic blurring wave—and they allowed me to sit up and cough out the bits of old tooth lodged in my gullet. Then we went back to it again. I bore it manfully for the next hour and a half giving a double thumbs up every time they asked me if I was okay.

I have new teeth. As I write this my top lip is frozen into a hard sneer and a passer-by might well think Billy Idol had let himself go, but my teeth look quite good. They're white but they're not too white. They're not the enormous overbite I was anticipating. They look good. I'm not sure you'd notice anything was different at all if you didn't know me well. They are not look-at-me teeth. They are humble, just-going-about-my-day-I-don't-want-any-trouble teeth.

I may even start smiling in photos now.

No. It looks weird. I'll continue to pout. It's all I know.

Today's oral surgery soundtrack included: Westlife, Dido, Kylie, Pink, and Nickelback, along with the alarming realisation that Cool FM has a dating site called, wonderfully, Cool FM Dating.

Just when you thought it was safe to go back in the water . . .

FIFTH APPOINTMENT

Nothing Dentured . . .

I ARRIVE at the Dentists. There's no one in reception. My Dentist appears and there's something different about him, something I can't quite put my finger on. Has he had some work done? A haircut? His face seems . . . longer. I realise this is the first time I've seen him without a mask. He has a bottom to his face. Lovely teeth. I wish I had his dentist.

I immediately go into a comic spiel—my defensive posture. It's been that way since I was a child—the bullies don't beat up the funny kid. School is hell. Survival of the funniest.

I start telling him about my dental adventures. When I came back from the dentist the last time, after I'd had my place-keeper front teeth installed, I admired the pristine whiteness that looked so strange in my mouth. I didn't want to eat with them but knew I would ultimately have to. I decided to compromise. I wouldn't eat actual food—I'd plump for a Pot Noodle.

It was a mistake. The Pot Noodle contained turmeric. Who knew that Pot Noodles had turmeric in them? They're basically fine dining. The upshot of this was that my brilliant, arctic smile was now a vibrant yellow, a banana Nesquik yellow, the yellow of an Eighties heavy metal drummer's headband. I was aghast. I'd spent thousands of pounds and had a white smile for less than an hour. It was like I'd thrown a lemon pop sock in with the white wash. Why hadn't the Dentist warned me? Why had he not specifically warned me not to eat Pot Noodles? I was paying him enough to cover every variable. I wanted a long list.

"Ah, yes," he said, "Turmeric will do that."

Apparently so.

I sat down in the chair and the glasses went on, the halo of lights shone in my eyes, a paper anti-drool bib placed around my neck (I assume that's what it's for) and business continued as usual in my distant, abstracted mouth. Dentistry is like that, or at least it is for me: I'm absent from it. Like an astral projection looking down on the doctor performing his surgery, I retreat. I vanish into the problem-solving areas of my brain, while my jaw vibrates, and a plastic straw sucks up pools of my saliva.

I was writing a short story. I had a man looking at the stalls in a Samhain Crafts Fair. I had about five pages of verisimilitude: the sticky-floored bar where it was taking place, the craft beers available, the contents of the stalls (mainly tote-bags and prints) and the people there (fun punk girls). My character would be a stranger, early to see a film in the next room and people-watching with a beer, until something draws him to one of the stalls.

But what was it? The rest of the story would obviously hinge on what that object was. And was I doing a magic object story? Like C. S. Lewis? Like *The Phantom Tollbooth*? Like *The Indian in the Cupboard*? (An aside: I'm surprised to find that book is not called *The Native American in the Cupboard* or *The First National in the Cupboard* now. It would seem an obvious thing to do and I think the former makes for a better title—it removes any lurking ambiguity. But It's still on Amazon as *The Indian in the Cupboard* and is listed as a "Teacher's Pick" as well. Odd. There are loads of sequels too, all banging on, inaccurately, about Indians).

Those are all children's books, but the story I'm writing is not. I'm looking for an object that could be found on a Bric-a-Brac stall that could open the story, something redolent of the past, something that might draw a clear line to the man's youth: a board game, perhaps? No, shades of *Jumanji*. How about a safe without a key? A Chinese box puzzle? A half-remembered book? A fifties vintage ray gun? X Ray Specs . . .

"Okay, Mr Higgins. I think that's you."

I snapped back into reality. Whatever they'd been doing to the inside of my head was complete. My mouth was still numb—I had a beak rather than lips—but I ran my tongue over a new row of smooth, even teeth. My bottom row was complete. I now had the place-holder teeth on top and this row of shiny, natural looking bottom teeth. I risked a smile into a proffered mirror. That was a smile. A proper smile. Clean, even, conventional teeth. I stopped smiling as I don't really know how. It looked odd, forced. But it was there if I needed it. It was a resource.

"What do you think?" said the Dentist.

"I'm beautiful," I said.

He didn't know whether to laugh, so he just nodded.

I paid the receptionist an enormous sum of money again, and she made a joke about it again, which she could easily afford to do. I went home to confront Susan with my smile. She was very complimentary, which is exactly what I wanted her to be. She never lets me down.

"Can you hear a slight speech impediment?" I said, when the anaesthetic had worn off and my mouth sunk back into its perma-sulk. Except I didn't say that. I said: "Can you hear rah shlight speech impuhdiment?"

"No," she lied.

But it was there.

My mouth got fairly used to the new teeth within a couple of days. But I still hear it, the same splashy sibilance is still there. And that's a sentence I'd rather not read out loud anymore.

UNEXPECTED SUPPLEMENTARY APPOINTMENT

IT WAS MY BIRTHDAY. Please do not ask how old I am. There are, I suppose, jokes to be made about my being "long in the tooth"—ha ha—though the truth of it is I'm very short on teeth indeed. I planned to do very little on my birthday. Susan and I would rise. I'd make my favourite breakfast: grilled tomato on sourdough with a splash of liquid wild garlic and a clove of garlic finely chopped and sprinkled on top. I have a jaded palette—I need something a bit lively to cut through with a mid-morning zing. I'd settle with a pot of Earl Grey, then start on the stack of presents in the corner of the room. There were a lot of gifts. In the past, a man of my years might have anticipated socks, or a pouch of pipe tobacco, perhaps a Len Deighton novel. Older men were self-sufficient, they didn't want fuss and silliness. They just wanted to be left alone with their PTSD and their dog, who was their best friend and the only one who understood them.

Bollocks to that. I'm Gen X—the Peter Pan generation. I want gifts. I desire shiny things. Bejewel me with baubles and festoon me with frivolities. I never grew up, and now I live surrounded by the things that obsessed me as a child: Polish film posters, phrenology heads, a globe that's also a drinks cabinet, a bust of Peter Cushing, a banker's lamp, a skull inkwell and loads of books about ghosts. I was a morbid child: pale and vitamin B deficient, staying in the house drawing superheroes on reams of computer paper. And after detouring into an adolescence and young manhood where I was ashamed of these things, I'm right back where I started: writing horror films under the watchful eye of a Green Man's big leafy face. I was very happy with my big pile of gifts and that took up most of the morning, after which I was peckish. So, I made a cheese sandwich.

A mistake.

There was a loud crack and something heavy and solid appeared in the bread and cheese mulch, something massive in the way objects found suddenly in your mouth feel gigantic, like someone parked a People Carrier in there. Susan heard the noise from across the room.

"Are you alright?"

I'm a past master of bits of my oral furniture just snapping off and falling out. It's happened to me all my life, despite the dedicated years of brushing, tooth whitening, and wearing gum shields, all those futile trips to the dentist. I knew what had happened. I fished out the weird tooth cladding. It was the upper left incisor. It came off in one piece, the tortional power necessary for bread and cheese defeating it.

"One of my incredibly expensive new teeth has come out." I said.

She gave me a look of infinite sadness, because she knows me and knew the next ten minutes were going to be unbearable. Whenever I lose a tooth, or a piece of tooth, or a filling or, on one occasion, a veneer I'd surrendered to a cheese souffle mere minutes after it had been applied, a part of me dies. There is the faintest shiver of mortality, a shadow over my grave. Something that was a part of me has been lost to eternity. A part of me is no longer part of my life, is no longer even alive. I feel it keenly. I am finite and can't afford to lose bits. I feel powerless, picked on, singled-out for special punishment. It was worse when I was poor because I couldn't do anything about it. I'd go to the dentist for my NHS check-up, she would investigate my quarry of a mouth, sigh, give the mouldering horrors a bit of a polish and send me on my way. That was all that could be done on the NHS. I trudged home.

One of the things you *can* do if your teeth need work, is ask to be referred to a teaching hospital where, in return for your signature, you'll be experimented on by a child with a drill. But even this didn't work—they couldn't do anything for me. After waiting six months on a referral list, I went home, unfixed.

It's not entirely about the teeth. Wrapped up in losing teeth are all the terrible decisions I've made or failed to make, the ones that left me poor and disenfranchised, and unable to pay for tooth-saving treatments. And it's a terrible reminder that the once-noble institution that is the National Health Service has been throttled and starved by successive Conservative governments, in a bid to keep affordable tooth-care out of the peasant mouths of people like me, who never vote for them and have no money, and therefore shouldn't exist.

There's the frisson of mortality, as bits of me crumble and fall away, but there's also the hysterical impulse that I can never shake, but which sees me flying into foot-stomping paroxysms of Rumpelstiltskin rage—my inner toddler demanding IT'S SO UNFAIR!

And this *was* doubly unfair. I'd paid for new teeth—ridiculous sums of money had flown out of my bank account—and they were still pinging out of my head into unassuming cheese sandwiches.

It was a Saturday. I couldn't even phone the dentist until Monday. So, I relaxed. I breathed. I centred myself. I didn't ruin the day. We cooked honey and lavender chicken (no, it's great) and I drank a bottle of Sauterne, and I didn't think about my teeth for the rest of the day. The little enamel brute had done its worst, but I'd been victorious. The day was saved.

I phoned on Monday and got an emergency appointment the next day. That's paying for stuff for you. You wouldn't get that on the bruised and battered NHS. You should though. I'd played into the Tory's manicured hands, their palms still bruised from clapping the NHS on their doorsteps during the pandemic. The NHS had saved Boris Johnson's life, and he just continued lying and partying and the Tories refused them a pay increase. Susan and I clapped along with everyone else, and she's a nurse, so we felt doubly stupid.

It was raining as I trudged the half-mile to the Dentist. I was not in my usual jocular mood. I had the rogue tooth in a small plastic baggie in my pocket. The Dentist appeared at the top of the stairs as usual, and we got on with it, without me doing my usual twenty minutes of people pleasing improv. God, I sicken me. When will it stop? I don't like the people who like me. Why would I need more? He's not going to charge me less for being his pal. There had been no mate's rates so far. If anything, he seemed to be adding treatments to the plan, to maximise his exposure to me. Like a psychopath would. They make good murderers, dentists. Hmm.

It seemed like an easy job. The tooth is all of a piece. It's just a matter of cementing it back into place. I lie back and he sticks some sort of clip around the tooth and speaks in code to his assistant. As usual I have very little idea what's happening. Time moves differently in the Dentist's chair. There are lights, intrusive fingers, masked strangers babbling. It seems likely to me that every alien abductee undergoing hypnosis is merely re-membering a long-repressed childhood visit to the dentist. Within ten minutes it's stuck in again and I'm sitting up, running my tongue over it. It feels the size of a sofa.

"Do you know, your denture came in early." He says "If you have time, we could fit it today. It'll only be twenty minutes or so."

I glower.

"Then again, if you're running late . . ." he trails off. But he has the thing in his hand. It's a denture, a proper one, with a pink gummy plate that will adhere to the roof of my mouth. And there are teeth attaching to it, occasional ones which I'm able to map onto the empty spaces. The appointment is for next Tuesday. I'm in no hurry to have a denture fitted.

"How does it fit in?" I say, "is there some sort of adhesive or something?"

"Oh, no. It's calibrated for the contours of your mouth. It'll just stay in place."

It's an impressive piece of work. The teeth look just like teeth. It strikes me we've never had a conversation about the colour of my new teeth. They look natural, not Hollywood beautiful, or that next step into spooky luminescence beloved of people who do red carpet interviews on cable channels you haven't heard of.

Still. Dentures.

"I can't believe I'm having a conversation about dentures," I say, "I'm a young man." The Dentist and Nurse both laugh, rather unnecessarily.

"But dentures. Sitting on my bedside table, fizzing away, like all my young dreams and aspirations . . ."

More laughter, but I'm not laughing. Dentures. The words of Pam Ayres' *Oh I Wish I'd Looked After My Teeth* haunt me in a moment: "As they foamed in the waters beneath." And that's what we're talking about: a cartoon of Granny's choppers grinning from a tumbler, tiny bubbles describing the grain of her celluloid molars. Or Les

Dawson shifting his bosom as a fearsome Northern matriarch, clacking his plate about when talking about his "downstairs" problems. We were talking about old age. My old age. The crumbling edifice of my body. The mouldering that comes before the grave. I was joking with them, but I was deadly serious.

"Is it going to affect my speech?" I said.

"It's a very tight-fitting mould; it should adhere very faithfully. And should feel comfortable and natural very quickly."

"So, it won't affect my speech?"

"No, it will. I encourage patients to practice reading out loud."

Excellent. Dentures *and* a speech impediment. Worth every penny. And suddenly I keenly felt the loss of each of those pennies, gone forever. I could have bought a perfectly adequate second-hand car. I could have gone on a holiday that looked like the holidays you see on TV, with white sand and Kanga skirts and smiling waiters in neat jackets trotting up to your sun lounger with cocktails, as opposed to three days in a budget hotel in a Medieval town looking at stained gargoyles, and sharing a flask of sachet coffee, which is our standard getaway. I could have had a suit made. Handmade Italian shoes. Hired a personal trainer, worked on the rest of me. I could have booked a suite on the *Orient Express* for a once-in-a-lifetime luxury train experience (and by the end of all this treatment I'll have spent enough to take Susan too). I could have handed a big cheque to a local charity and pouted on the steps of a crumbling prefabricated library in a local newspaper. I could have launched any number of vanity projects: recorded an album, authored a slim volume of poetry. An exhibition of my accomplished paintings. But I didn't do these things. I spent the money on a set of dentures and a speech impediment.

The other thing bothering me was: was I going to be charged for this? I mean, he had fitted the tooth and the tooth had broken in a fortnight. Surely, he couldn't expect me to pay again. Was I going to have to make a scene? Sadly, I'm one of those English people who doesn't know how to make a scene. I've never been one for saying "I don't want to talk to you, I want to talk to the manager", because I've been a lifelong underling and know how that feels. But I'm also full of simmering rage, probably because of a lifetime of dealing with those people, so I'm either passive-aggressive—"No, fine. If *that's* what you think. If that's what you think *is fair* . . . FINE,"—or I'm the Hulk. I don't look like the Hulk—I'm puce and weedy, but my reasoning is the Hulk's. Ugly teeth are gnashed, brows are furrowed white, and I start stamping that foot again. I wish there were a third way, because neither of these approaches helps me in any way.

He doesn't mention any money. I confirm the next appointment and walk straight out. I'm expecting a phone call saying "Hey, sorry, you owe me a shit-ton of cash," as I walk home in the rain, as usual. But it never comes. I've got away with it. For now.

The Dentist is keen. Each time I make an appointment, I get a little card with my appointment on it. It's followed up with an e-mail. The day before the appointment I get another reminder e-mail, and the receptionist rings and leaves a voicemail asking me to call her and confirm I can still make the appointment the following day. I have never phoned her. Susan thinks this is bad manners, but I've made that appointment and will keep it. If I can't keep it, I will let them know, but I don't expect to have to take the time to confirm that I'll be keeping the appointment I've made. I'm just going to keep it. That's enough, right? Should I ring them as I'm leaving the house on the day of the appointment to give them my E.T.A? Give or take a few minutes depending on traffic/my tiredness/the tightness of my shoes?

I might do this.

Something . . . something . . . the root of all evil . . . something . . .

ADVENTURES IN DENTURES

HE SHORT FILM I'm making is coming to a head. The final thing to do is the design of the inter-titles. The producers are very busy across multiple projects, and the only time they can find to argue about them is when I'm in the Dentist's chair. To be fair to them I have been in the Dentist's chair quite a lot recently. I'm having dentures fitted today.

Dentures. I still can't get my head around the idea that I'm going to have dentures. And a speech impediment—he's promised me that. They just throw that in.

The waiting room is unusually full. A red-haired woman is politely shocked by the prices the jaded receptionist is quoting her. A nun descends the staircase. You don't get many nuns in East Belfast. She looks like a ghost and when she speaks it's like a draft rising through cellar doors. Brides of Christ. Poor Christ.

Even the potted plant looks depressed today. It needs two bamboo sticks to prop it up. Its wide, dusty leaves look like sick tongues. Say "Aaaah". *Teenage Dirtbag* plays. A denture. I'm getting a denture. I'm just an elderly dirtbag, baby.

I bound up the stairs to visit the Dentist's room. I'm wearing trainers and a band t-shirt but I'm being fitted for a pair of dentures. I'm fooling no one. This is an unusual appointment as I've not had my jaw frozen. It should be quick and straightforward. And I can keep my glasses on.

The Dentist whips out the dentures and wedges the upper one over my teeth. It's tight, gripping my teeth in a way that seems alien to me—traditionally, I've avoided taking risks with pressure on my teeth because my teeth have not been up to the task. He takes it out again and there's the sound of something abrasive being worked over the plate. Even though I can see this time, I still don't look at what he's doing. Something comes over me in the Dentist's chair. I become oblivious to everything that's going on around me, like it's not my business. Anything could be happening, and I'll just be staring into the bright lights, like a character from a Jay McInerney novel.

He sticks the upper plate in again. It's tight but it fits. He pops in the lower plate. The two plastics discs are clipped on. It's like having an internal beak. The roof of my mouth is smooth, inhuman, and my mouth is suddenly a lot smaller. The Nurse hands me a mirror.

I have perfect teeth. Two rows of pristine white teeth. For the first time since my twenties. It looks odd. I look like the actor playing me in a Hallmark movie of my life.

"What do you think? I'm very pleased with the fit."

It looks perfect. There are no tell-tale bits of metalwork holding it in. It's invisible mending.

"It'shh amazzhing," I say. Ah, there it is. The speech impediment, as promised. It better not show up on my bill.

"You're going to have that until your mouth adjusts," he says. I'm not sure my mouth is ever going to adjust to having two coasters wedged in there. But I speak slowly and my tongue hits slightly different parts of my mouth, and very quickly my speech is almost back to normal.

"I'm going to ask you to remove and replace the false teeth now," he says.

"Woah! Don't call them 'false teeth'. Never call them 'false teeth'. Denture is bad enough, but I'm not having anyone call them 'false teeth'. My God!"

He doesn't call them false teeth again, and I flip out the top set.

"Like this?"

"Yes, very good. Could you pop them back in?" I do it in a single fluid motion.

"Like this?"

"Yes. Okay, people aren't normally as good at doing it that quickly. Well done."

What a skill to have. Good at putting my dentures in, and never had one lesson. My whole life has been leading to this moment. Finally, I am good at something and its false teeth.

He advises me on taking care of them, cleaning them, and presents me with a blue plastic box to store them in. It's shaped like a coffin. I mean . . .

I pay the receptionist another enormous sum of money and head off to the opticians to pick up some contact lenses. I remind myself of a Victorian "Vinegar Valentine", the charming custom of sending ugly people reminders of their ugliness every 14th February. One showed a woman standing before a mirror and bore the legend "False thou art . . ." and listed her fake beauty spot, her wig, her glass eye, her wooden leg. And that's me wandering off to pick up contact lenses with a mouth full of plastic teeth—false thou art. Maybe I'll pick up some "Just For Men" while I'm about it.

At the optician, a man approaches and asks, "Can I help you, pal?" and, because he's from Belfast, it *does* sound like a threat.

"I'm here to pick up some contact lenses," I say. It sounds okay. I sound normal. I flash him a grin and immediately stop, as I don't quite know the wattage of my smile. I don't want to dazzle him.

"Sure, pal, what's the name?"

"Bwon Hyurgensss,"

"Come again, pal?"

"Dyong Higgeenth," I manage. I can't say my own name. This might prove tricky. It stands as a black-mark against the dentures, though the biggest black-mark against the dentures is they're dentures.

I procure the contact lenses by pointing and smiling. I assume they think I've had some sort of head injury on the way to the shop—when the optician asks me if I want the lenses initialled "L" and "R" I give her a thumbs up and another fluorescent smile. I pick up some Steradent from a Pound Shop on the way home, because that's just who I am now.

At home Susan is supportive as ever. I spend time looking at my rows of perfect teeth in the mirror and she tells me they look great, and I have a lovely smile. I read to her, trying to discover where to put my tongue in my new tiny plastic mouth, so I can shape the sounds of letters properly, and she reads to me about how my mouth will produce more saliva initially because there's a foreign object in it, and I tell her she's right and swallow another great gobbet of spit.

I eat dinner with my false teeth. It's a lasagne. It's the first time I've had molars in my head for a very long time, and I attempt to chew with them. The whole thing feels strange, and I feel the pressure of the fake teeth biting into my gums. The mince gets everywhere and five minutes after finishing I'm rinsing lumps of semi-masticated meat off my plate. Glamour.

After a week I'm not getting on with the dentures. I still have cuts on my gums from the lower set. I've learned to speak well with them—though the word "superstitious" is a challenge—but mostly the words sound okay, despite the persistent denture whistle. Susan tells me she can't hear it, but I can hear it. The teeth fit well; they don't slip. But they become uncomfortable after a few hours. They do look good, and I think if I had to commit to them, if I had no other options, I might learn to get on with them. People the world over have dentures and they're fine with them. What makes me so special with my prissy little pink gums? But I'm many, many thousands of pounds in the hole on this dental journey, and I did not start out with the objective of having false teeth. This seems like an unnecessary distraction on my journey to a workable smile. It's depressing. The tawdry ritual of it all: taking the plates out of their little plastic tub. Watching the Steradent tablet fizzing blue in its glass. Washing them gently. Clipping them into my mouth and wincing at the sensitivity. Clenching them in the mirror and noting they do look good. They look like normal teeth until I attempt to talk or eat. I see people on adverts biting into crisp, pink apples with their dentures. I don't think so. They look good but they're not fit for my purpose.

I'm experiencing a sunk cost: I have invested too much in my teeth to stop now. I'm like a Trump supporter watching each new outrage and thinking, well I better stick with this guy regardless, I already got the MAGA tattoo.

I'm probably going to get implants, though they're ridiculously expensive: for the price of three I could buy a Skoda Yeti Mk1. I don't want to, but I could. But I've a need for a viable, cutlery drawer full of clean, efficient teeth that are fully attached to my head. I've told too many people I'm doing this. I *haven't* told them how much it's costing.

Reactions to the work I've had done already have been muted at best. My friend Joe said: "Oh, you have white teeth," and left it at that. My friend Shauna said, despite knowing I'd been having cosmetic dentistry for weeks, "I've never looked at your teeth. I don't think people really notice teeth."

But *I* noticed my teeth. And maybe that's the point here. This smile is for me. I may never use it, but I'd like to know it's there, like life insurance or an erection. I'd like at least one marker of visible decrepitude to have been held off. Who knows where this will end? Gastric bands? A tushy tuck? Having my balls lifted? I'm not even sure that last one is a thing, but I bet some unscrupulous doctor somewhere has promised a scrotum-dysmorphic patient, "No problem. Step into this backless gown and lie face-down on the slab". Anal bleaching. That really *is* a thing. A mysterious thing. Whose anus is so regularly scrutinised they think "Hmm. If I could lighten that to a sort of cornflake tan, I'd show my poop-chute off to its full advantage". But maybe that's what happens when the madness takes hold, a fist waved at the sky to an uncaring God who allowed you to become imperfect. Soon you're having your navel re-shaped ("teardrop is very in, sir,") or having ribs removed to make autofellatio a reality.

I've earmarked a certain amount of money for my teeth. And that is all I shall be spending on them. I know this, as I have taken the clever precaution of not having any more money to spend after I've spent it.

Smart.

I should try and get on better with the dentures. I've paid for them after all. I think I was expecting after a week, for them to feel natural and comfortable, that my speech would be clear and that I'd be experiencing the peculiar delight of chewing with a working molar. But after a week they still hurt. My gums are raw. The chewing makes me very aware of their plasticity. After three or four hours I'm longing to take them out again.

APPOINTMENT 6

(Or 7, Depending on How You're Counting. I'll Say 6)

"So how are you getting on?"

"Yeah, not bad. Bit of a bad back."

"With the dentures?"

Oh right. Of course.

We're pretty pally me and the Dentist, but our meetings tend to be fairly orally fixated.

"Can I see?"

I'm not wearing the dentures. After a slow start, I have been wearing them for six or seven hours every day. They still hurt but only when I first fit them, and then only the bottom set. The excessive drooling has abated, and the speech impediment is something only I seem to notice, though to my ears I sound like I'm always talking into a tea pot. As today's project is to take the temporary caps off my front teeth, take moulds of the stubs underneath and then replace the temporary caps again, while the moulds go off to make my final crowns, I didn't think I needed to wear the dentures at all. I assumed they would get in the way. The Dentist looks perturbed.

"We can work around it, I suppose." He seems put out. "How are you getting on with them?"

"Not great," I say, "they're less uncomfortable than they used to be, but I'm still not really eating with them, after an early mishap with a lasagne. Then there's the ritual of cleaning them with soap and a baby toothbrush, rinsing away the blue water of the Steradent tablet—which, disturbingly, is also very good for cleaning the toilet—and leaving them there overnight in their tub. But mainly it's about my self-image. I don't want to be someone with dentures. I'm only fifty. Dentures belong on the bedside cabinet of snoring grandpa with a David Baldacci novel steepling on his chest. That's not me. I'm a stylish man about town, not a shivering shut-in sharing a tin of cat food with an equally decrepit moggie. I'm still young."

The Nurse was again surprised to hear I was young and emitted a nervous laugh.

"Also, they make my gums bleed. You can have a look."

He did, brusquely identifying the spot with his little lollypop mirror.

"They shouldn't be cutting your gums. We can adjust them next time you come in. Ideally, you'd have been wearing them today, but we can work round it."

And with that the Nurse draped a paper apron round my neck and the radial lights dazzled me again. I was expecting to be in the chair for perhaps twenty minutes. It was the simple matter of breaking off my front teeth, making a mould of my stumps, and sticking some fresh teeth back on. Simple. A mindless thug could do it. Already had done.

I was in the chair for an hour and a half. During that time, I heard the phrase, "There's going to be a little tap—nothing Medieval", which is exactly what you want to hear your dentist say. There followed a cross between Woody Woodpecker at his most irritating and Hugh Grant's percussive finale in *Paddington 2*. It was a surfeit of taps—a plumber's odds 'n' sods drawer of taps. More taps than an American military funeral.

Eventually the temp teeth were off, and I was asked to bite on a series of what appeared to be slivers of malleable metal, as though he were cooking them al dente and needed reassurance. Then came the moulds. Both upper and lower teeth were moulded. And this was strange—he'd taken moulds of my teeth before the original temporary caps went on. What was wrong with those moulds? And if the fidelity to the tooth stumps was compromised by putting the temps on, surely that would happen again? I wasn't party to the mysterious activities in my mouth. I was forced to lie back and think of England. And then, after a few seconds and a shiver, some less divisive country. I find my acquiescence in these experiments disturbing. I will go along with anything, so long as someone in scrubs and a plausible manner tells me it's necessary. I would have easily been tricked into becoming a human centipede—I'd just assume the mad scientist had my best interests at heart: "You want to sew my mouth to his what now?" "My diet will be mostly what? Okay, Doc. You're the boss!"

I sneered at anti-vaxxers—rightly—but at least they ask *questions*. Stupid, stupid questions, but still questions. So, what if they think that 5G makes their uterus shrivel, or the Covid vaccine will turn your knees French, at least they're not just *taking* it, compliant and supine, like a prison wife who's given up the fight.

For an hour and a half I drifted off, while a plastic lip divider was placed in my mouth and the assistant hovered with that spit-sucking device that never works, while the Dentist chiselled off my teeth, got me to bite on strips of metal with my broken stumps, placed metal discs of varying sizes in my mouth, took moulds of all my teeth. Other people came in, wandered around. I assumed they were other dentists or dental nurses, but they could have been members of the public paying to gawp at the human zoo—then he reapplied the same fake front teeth or attached different fake front teeth. Meanwhile I was thinking about titles for a short film I'm planning, and the lyrics for a song I'd started writing in the waiting room. Anything to avoid being there, my mouth clamped open, blue rubber fingers rummaging, shifting the furniture. Finally, I was allowed to sit up, and the Nurse handed me a mirror. I had a welt between my eyes from the sunglasses and my mouth was pink and stretched from the dental guard. I had bits of dental matter all over my face and clothes. At that point he requested a photo.

"Could you smile into the camera, teeth apart, showing your top and bottom row?" said David Hamilton. I was imagining him draping gauze over the lens. "It's to show them what your smile is supposed to look like." I expect I look like somebody who's staggered from a traffic accident amazed to still be alive, I thought. He snapped away.

"There's one for your wallet!" I said. Hoots of laughter, with panic edging in mine. That was the worst appointment since the extractions. I looked rattled in the mirror, my voice cracking with hysteria. The next appointment was a month away. Was that recovery time?

"Make sure you wear your dentures for that one."

Downstairs I approached reception, my wallet already in my hand, and confirmed the next appointment. She handed me an appointment card and I waited. Her smile froze, then slipped off like ice from a garage roof.

"You okay?"

"How much do I owe you?"

"Nothing."

"Nothing?"

"That's what I said. Nothing."

"Are you sure?"

She stared testily at her computer screen.

"No, nothing here. If you're giving away money . . ." this last accompanied by a mirthless bark.

"No, you're alright. Bye."

My phone was in my thigh pocket. They'd done this to me before. On this occasion I had to go to the optician to get a replacement lens, as I'd scratched my glasses attempting an alfresco wee in a thornbush. It's not something I would ordinarily do, but I have two rituals which I live by everyday: I drink a large pot of Earl Grey tea, and I go for a two-hour walk. On this occasion, a conjunction of the two events found me hiding in the bushes, and cocking an ear for passing joggers. When I emerged from the scrub, I found cuts all over the back of my right hand, and the light flaring in my left eye like I was watching a JJ Abrams film. The scratch was large and descended across the lens, like a depressed clown's autograph.

A trip to the optician. Sixty pounds for a lens replacement. When I spend a penny, I go all out. The whole time I was there I was expecting the phone in my thigh pocket to vibrate, to be summoned back to the dentist to settle. I went to Poundland and bought more Steradent denture cleaner from a beautiful 25-year-old girl. Sigh. Still nothing. I walked home. No call. I'd got away with it.

Who am I kidding. They're biding their time. They know where I live.

My new temporary cap falls out. I'm eating salad. Salad is too much for my beleaguered gnashers now. It's fully five days since I had the tooth put in. It is also the same tooth that fell out last time. Today is the Sunday of a Bank Holiday, meaning the dentist will be closed tomorrow, the earliest I can call is on Tuesday, and the earliest he'll see me will be Wednesday. Three days with this grey stump of a tooth with, I note, some of the cement still clinging to it. Luckily, I have no social life at all, so I can cling to the shadows, twitching at curtains, living that Boo Radley dream. It does rather shake my confidence in my teeth, however. Once again, I'm forced to conclude that I'm multiple thousands of pounds into this process, and I have a painful denture and some temporary caps that aren't up to the challenge of feta cheese.

APPOINTMENT NUMBER . . . I'VE LOST TRACK BY THIS POINT

The Puns Seem To Have Dried up Too

IN FACT, the Dentist is on holiday, so it's a week and a half before I can get an appointment. There's something I failed to disclose earlier when I mentioned losing my temp incisor to a bowl of salad.

When I came home from the Dentist last time, I put the denture over my new replacement tooth. The geography of my mouth had clearly changed, and it was a struggle to get the top set to adhere to the roof of my mouth. They are very bespoke false teeth, and the tiniest molar miscalculation puts them out of whack and, as I pushed the bridge against the roof of my mouth, there was a huge cracking noise. I froze. I'm all too familiar with the sound of my teeth snapping and crumbling out of my mouth, and this had the electric horror of one of those moments. I've broken a thousand pounds worth of denture, I thought, retrieving it from my mouth and expecting it to come out in two neat parts, like a toastie from a Breville Sandwich maker. It emerged intact. Shit. It must be the teeth. I did a quick inventory and was surprised to find everything accounted for. Odd. The loud cracking noise in my mouth was . . . nothing. Two days later my tooth fell out in a Greek salad. Clearly, I'd cracked the tooth and it was just waiting for the excuse of a few Mediterranean leaves to exit my mouth. And that's the story I told the dentist, as I sat back, once again in his chair, as familiar to me now as the bum-groove of my own sofa.

I had the dentures in this time so he could see them in situ. I hadn't worn them for a week and was dreading putting them in as they'd cut my gums, particularly the lower set. I was looking forward to pointing out the gouges in my gums—look what you've done, dentist, I'm in ribbons. But they were the most comfortable they'd ever been. They slipped on like old slippers. It was infuriating.

He looked tanned. He'd been to Tenerife. He also seemed taller. The trousers of his scrubs were only down to his shins, as though all the good living had led to a mid-life growth spurt. He exuded health and vitality. Whereas I now produced a tooth from a baggie in my pocket.

"I brought it from home."

"Are you wearing the dentures?" he said, laser focused. I flashed the plastic at him.

"How do they feel?"

"They're the most comfortable they've ever been," I said, pouting. "Been away?"

That got him.

"Ah yes," he said, "I was on holiday. Sorry, otherwise I'd have got to your teeth a bit sooner. Apologies."

I'd made him apologise for his holiday. This was good.

"Anywhere nice?"

"Tenerife. Five hours on the plane. Mad. You'd think it was just off the coast of Spain, but . . ."

"No, it isn't," I said. I have no idea where Tenerife is. But he didn't know that. He glued the tooth back in. Then he started shaving down the denture to accommodate the new tooth. A couple of fittings later it was perfect. The conversation moved onto the American Writer's Strike currently choking film production. I say the conversation "moved onto" but in fact what happened was I said "This bloody writer's strike . . ."

The writer's strike affects me. The film script I'd been working on for the last couple of years had been through four different re-writes, and the producers appeared pleased enough to forward it to the studio executives. What happens next will be one of two things: the studio will demand notes, I will be unable to provide them without becoming a scab, and everything will shudder to a halt. Or they won't require re-writes, and the film may push into production sooner rather than later—there's no director's strike after all. People *pay* directors.

It'll be the former. The idea of studio bosses not demanding arbitrary changes because they can is unthinkable.

I feel a warm bond of solidarity for my fellow poorly rewarded scribes. We were already downtrodden and disregarded and now we're going to be replaced by A.I. You think people will care? People won't care. Day time TV is already chockfull of films that betray no hint of humanity. But really, the *timing!* The last writer's strike lasted eighteen months! I want to get my debut feature made before I'm eligible for a bus pass. It's already been dragging on for a couple of years. I really haven't got time for these glacial progressions. I'm already old. This film was supposed to be my leverage, my bartering chip. You get success by being successful, yes, but even if the film isn't successful, you get to make another thing by *having made a first thing*. In this industry the idea that you're only as good as your last film doesn't really apply. You just need to have done *something*. So, I would really like to get my film made.

As I explain this to the Dentist, he starts to look genuinely upset, and I realise that no one ever gets this worm's-eye-view of the film industry. We know the success stories, we don't hear the fuck ups, probably because the noise would be deafening. Hollywood is built on hope, on giving away free shit, on being swindled and, above all, on failure. Though that's the lot of the writer everywhere, not just in films. And he's been given all this staggering new information from a middle-aged man with a shock of grey hair and fifteen teeth less than he was born with.

"It's shocking," he says, "the lack of control you have, the lack of power . . ."

I'm not sure if I need to hold him. His world has been rocked. I wasn't expecting empathy from a man who has been extracting both teeth and pounds from me over the last five months. My cynical girlfriend suggested he was worried I wouldn't be able to pay him anymore, but he seemed genuinely moved by the plight of jobbing scribbler, not something many people are bothered by, as they assume the Netflix series they binge on are spontaneous flowers of nature, blooming unbidden into their living rooms.

I have looked into the eyes of the Dentist and found a fellow human being. As I go, he escorts me down the stairs and out the door. He seems on the cusp of slapping me on the back. The moment goes.

I feel good. The sun the sun is shining. I've been walking a lot recently and feel stronger and healthier than I have for some time. The warmth of the day irons out the kinks in my spine. It pops like bubble wrap as I straighten. I buy some sausages.

I get into the moment. It's been raining, but the sun is hot now, and swirling curlicues of steam are dancing on the wet tarmac. I've never seen that before and feel buoyed by the strange phenomena of the world about me. My dentures feel fine. They're comfortable and I start to affect a roguish smile, casually, as though I were remembering an incorrigible young manhood, while carrying a bag of sausages. I walk past a shop window. Have I lost weight? Have I gained height? My posture is magnificent. Then there are the teeth, gleaming out of the darkness like a penny down a wishing well. They look *good*. I have a smile again. I throw my head back and walk home, beaming.

There's a building site near my home. Over the last few months, I've watched the slow progress of a house being built. The foundations were laid around the same time I began to get my teeth fixed, the two projects running in tandem. The house is arguably more impressive, bigger—certainly. But there have been divers hands working on that project: architects planning it, local councillors—pockets stuffed with brown envelopes—allowing it, property developers paying off the councillors, and an army of workmen to build it. My teeth are just me and the Dentist and, if I'm honest, he's doing most of the work. Bricks and mortar don't need healing time.

There are three builders working on it today as I stroll past, grinning. Builders have changed. In my day they were big, ruddy chaps in baggy corduroys and flat caps, smoking cigarettes and always showing a good four inches of bum cleavage. They'd clamber around rusted scaffolding, screaming good-natured sexual abuse at passing women, and good-natured asexual abuse at me. They were the dowdy great apes of metropolitan renewal: grunting, flinging their shit, and demanding tea parties under little candy-striped canvas tents.

But these builders weren't like that at all. They were in their twenties, ripped and lean, scampering with animal grace over the rubble, standing on some promontory, the warm breeze in their hair like the Monarch of the Glen with a sleeve of tattoos. There was no fat on them, no body hair. Brave, certain and nimble, they'd never broken a bone, never felt the sudden slap of gravity. They were young and confident and proud of their tits. I felt a cloud pass over the sun. I sank with the sadness of a dropped accordion, my grey head lolling. My body was like furry dough, balanced on brittle breadstick legs and mocked by the builder's careless grace. I felt old. I felt mortal. I'd seen my replacements and realised I was no longer fit for purpose. The pearliest smile in the world couldn't change that.

Was that what all of this had been for? I'd been carrying around those stained and broken teeth as a *memento mori*, the way the merchant's skull slants through the painting by Holbein. Teeth are all you can see of your skeleton, a glimpse of bare skull. And my bones were rotting, mouldering as if already in the grave. In replacing them, I was replacing my youth. And you can't.

I'd seen those luminous smiles gleaming from the wizened, tandoori faces of elderly celebrities, their sunglasses hiding myriad sins, their hair in unlikely clumps, coconut coarse, their throats a tangled rope ladder and a dead giveaway. I'd sneered when I was younger, spat at their tragic vanity, their knotted claws clutching after past glories. No, not past glories. Youth. The golden ichor. The sweetness and suppleness, the easiness of youth.

Getting out of bed in the morning and having no idea what the day will bring, but knowing that clean limbs, a flat stomach, a firm jaw and shiny white teeth will be a match for anything thrown at you. That's what they want, the celebrities, while knowing they can never get it. They make do with the illusion of youth, mostly a ghastly mockery of it. But slap enough Vaseline over the camera's lens and the fillers, the brittle hair, the pristine smile might be enough to fool you.

I went home and tried to explain this to Susan. But it came out as an inarticulate existential howl, so we had a cup of tea. Because we're English and that's what we do.

I try to eat a sausage sandwich with the dentures in. The space of my mouth has shrunk, the two plastic discs of my plate confusing me as I attempt to swallow, and there's a slight panic as I feel like I might swallow the denture even though its firmly affixed. I choke back a lot of air too. I take the dentures out and nibble at the remaining sandwich with my temporary capped teeth.

I'll try again with the dentures. But I know that my heart isn't in it. I don't want *false teeth*.

PENULTIMATE APPOINTMENT

(Or Is It)

THE RECEPTIONISTS are having lunch in the back room, with the door open. They barely look up when I come in now.

"That's alright, John. Just take a seat."

They return to their conversation. One of them says, "I think that's one of my toxic behaviours: taking things and not giving them back."

That's one word for it.

I decide not to take a seat and instead head to the toilet. I'm early for my appointment, because I'm always early for my appointment. There's a motion sensor in the toilet. As I stand there, concentrating, drawing a bead on the Armitage Shanks, I'm plunged into darkness. Luckily, I wasn't mid-stream. I waggle my arms about a bit and the lights come back on.

How is this a good idea? Who's dancing in the toilet? I was standing there for no more than ten seconds be-

fore the lights went out. That's not a long time to success-
fully complete this transaction, and I'm standing. What
if you were sitting down, shitting into the sudden darkness? The whole thing seems like a recipe for sallow lino
and spending on bleach what you save on lightbulbs.

This is my penultimate appointment. I'm getting my
temporary caps off, my final teeth positioned onto my
ragged stumps, photographed, and then another set of
temps attached while the final-boss, end-game teeth are
refined by "the boys down at the lab". That's what I was
told was going to happen anyway.

There's a relaxed ambience in the surgery. It's surprisingly jolly and convivial considering that in a few
minutes my teeth are going to be smashed in. It's like en-
joying the craic in the moments leading up to a punishment beating. We get onto *Father Ted*—I'm not sure how—
and the Dentist says, a little ruefully, that *Father Ted* is so
old that he meets people who no longer understand *Father Ted* references, and I have visions of him breaking the
ice at dentist parties by pouring the wine and repeating,
"Ah Go On, Go On . . . just the glass in your hand." The
long winter evenings must fly by.

The Nurse admits that she is one of those people,
which makes me feel very old, and I try out a couple in
a shaky Irish accent: "Ah Ted, you big fool!" "Doesn't it

look like a face?" "It's the largest lingerie department in Europe, so I understand." But my dive into Craggy Island deep cuts was starting to alienate the Dentist as well, so I bit my tongue. The Nurse was already talking about her husband being the opposite of her—he knew all about TV: "He has the biggest collection of films in the world."

I wasn't having that.

"You should see my house. Wall to wall DVDs. I've even still got my videos, some of them." This drifted into a conversation about outmoded media generally, and I told them that like vinyl, cassettes were making a comeback—hipsters liked them—and that a friend had issued a couple of experimental albums on cassette, because I like people to know I'm the sort of guy who knows people who release experimental music on cassette.

The Dentist then pulled the rug from under me: my proper teeth were in. He would be able to apply them today. I would be walking home with the finished articles.

It was all over in no time. The build-up of the previous six months, the extraction of half my mouth, lacing up the wounds, the pink tinged brine drinks, the mini-oil derricks mounted on my gums, the endless circumlocution of that spit-guzzling pipe that does nothing, the fake teeth, unsegmented, like a gum shield, like an ashtray, going on, coming off, going on, coming off again—

the fucking dentures fizzing in their blue coffin-shaped box—and I was finally here. I had my new teeth.

I ran my tongue over them. Unlike the built-up bottom teeth, a lumpen, blunted mass, these felt like teeth. Real teeth. As much as I could remember what having real, clean, straight, individual teeth felt like. It had been nearly twenty years since that junkie in my hallway knocked them out of my head.

But you don't forget, not really. You know when something is right. And I had proper teeth again. Slender, strong, firmly rooted teeth. Air passed between them with a whistle. The nurse handed me a mirror and I gave a tentative smile, my lips noticeably dry and loose from a surfeit of rubber-gloved fingering.

I had a smile.

It was white, it was clean, it was even. There was the sense of an overbite. These were the teeth of my young manhood. This is what my teeth used to be like. I had the smile of a 21-year-old. It looked perverse surrounded by the grey, jowly face of a middle-aged man. I watch myself smiling into the Nurse's mirror. I have apple cheeks. Rosy, red, perfectly round cheeks and perfect white teeth. I look like a jolly cartoon beaver. I stop smiling.

"What do you think?"

"They're nice."

I fear I'm not giving him what he needs. We've been on a long journey together. There should be tears. Is he expecting a hug? I'm English—I wasn't even going to go with a firm, businesslike handshake. I pick up the mirror again. They look beautiful. Not showy. Natural. Actual human teeth that you might be born with and still have at fifty if you'd never heard of Coca Cola. My eyes start to glitter. Oh God. It's happening. I'm crying at my teeth. The dentist and the assistant look on, beaming under their masks. I feel like I'm nursing a newborn for the sake of the midwives.

"Thank you so much. They're beautiful."

"I think they've really worked out well. I'm very pleased."

I contemplate the handshake, but the moment is gone yet again. Besides he's from Northern Ireland and therefore even more emotionally numb than I am. Should I slap him on the back? I just go down and pay the final bill, which is fully a third again of all the monies I've already spent, and I walk off into the street, smiling aggressively at bus queues and school children. I make it home without being arrested.

Susan loves the teeth. She keeps asking me to smile for her, taking in the angles, the glint of the white. My cheeks hurt. I look like a Gibb brother you never heard about, or a forgotten Osmond. One of the deaf ones. The front teeth are perfect, but there are spaces behind them when I grin broadly. Maybe I could get a couple of implants there. They're only a few thousand each. Maybe one below, so I could have, like, a molar.

And I think of Michael Jackson, Lola Ferrari, or Mickey Rourke, who has turned his head into a sentient saddle. This is how it starts. You could, realistically, go on forever. Go on till the money runs out. I look at my grey hair, my pendulous jowls, like panniers on a bike, the faded eyebrows and lashes, my elephant's knee of a forehead. My face is not worthy of these beautiful teeth. It'll all have to change, all of it. It'll all have to come out. Dyes, tinctures, fillers, nips, tucks. I'll have my balls tightened—how can I wear skinny jeans with these low hanging fruit? An extra kneecap mid-thigh. My love of restaurant quality food and sommelier approved wine, together with the hangover 20th Century cool I'm forced to carry with me everywhere—the only weightlifting I allow myself—makes me sneer at spandex, at effort, at the horrors of gym culture, of the powders you consume. The smell of it. The conversations you'd overhear on the treadmill. The fucking awful music. The would-be-spiritual, wholistic, nasty-namaste Goop-iness of it all. An intersection between hippies and bros who are into their bodies is the most insidious intersection I can imagine. The gym is like being stuck at a garden party with the worst people in the world, but the garden is inside, and it smells of ass and everyone is a right-wing conspiracy theorist now. I'll take the surgery every time, expiring on the operating table with a beatific, perfectly engineered smile.

Not really. Maybe I could take up pilates again. It's a license to fart in public. And I really like the lavender eye-pillows.

A couple of days before my final treatment, I went on holiday. On the second morning of the holiday, I woke and blearily checked my phone, to find I had been offered a publishing contract for my first novel. There's no better way to start a holiday, or a day, or the rest of my life, quite frankly. It is no more or less than a longed-for dream come true.

It was a long e-mail, and I skimmed it—saw the word "unfortunately"—in shocking neon—and assumed it was a brush off. Nevertheless, I returned to the beginning, reading it properly and with mounting disbelief. They loved the manuscript. LOVED IT. The publisher told me he mostly read it in a library and was embarrassed by how often he'd had to laugh out loud. HAD TO, is the clincher here. It *is* a comedy, so unanswerable laughter is key. I read the e-mail to Susan, my voice high and girlish, as it is when suffused with glee, and her hands clasped in front of her, her smile beaming, the light in her beautiful eyes. She radiated joy. It was a good start to the holiday.

The only person as thrilled about the news as Susan (and myself) was the Dentist. He'd been worried about my travails with the Hollywood Writer's Strike, so he was thrilled I'd been thrown this lifeline. I had to sit down and tell him the realities of being a writer once again. There's likely no money in it, the possibility of secondary opportunities coming off the back of it is ever present, but financial security is far from guaranteed and every published writer I know has a day job. He looked mildly traumatised.

"The way you talk about it . . . it sounds so depressing. So, sort of precarious."

Hey! I got a publisher. It's an answer to a dream, and all I had to do was work hard for several years for no reward and with no guarantee of any success, while I was the poorest I'd ever been in my adult life. This is a happy day. Don't rain on my pomade, tooth butcher. I was overjoyed. As I left, I flashed him a radiant smile, which I was well able to do now.

Outside the sun was shining, but not as dazzlingly as my oral furniture, which had the brilliance of a low winter sun. My journey was done.

That's my teeth fixed. Now to ruin absolutely everything else . . .

SMILES FROM NOWHERE

THE REACTION to my exquisite smile has been . . . subdued. I went out to a gig the other day, expecting people to ask me to smile like it was my party piece, as though I were performing a dazzling piece of close-up magic. "Oh my God, John. do that again. It's amazing. Hey everybody come and look—John's doing stuff with his mouth!" Nobody noticed at all. Eventually *I* brought it up—I didn't want to, I don't want to be a tooth bore—but it was a huge deal for me, the culmination of six months of complex and committed cosmetic surgery, and it was getting *nothing*. So, I brought it up, even offering to smile for my friends, which felt so wrong. I haven't smiled for decades. I'm grin-shy. It felt like getting the old chap out and waving it around in the pub. Nevertheless, I WAS proud of the freshly minted sparklers, so I assayed a few smiles, running the gamut from smirk to full Joker.

Nothing. Shrugs. Nervous smiles. A coughed "Very nice."

Sigh.

If someone bought a pair of knock-off Aviators from a covered market, you'd make positive noises. If they'd purchased a couple of Ben Sherman shirts from Primark and gave you the price, you'd nod and smile and tell them how clever they were to get such a bargain (if not the Ben Shermans). If a friend unveiled a tattoo, still pink and sore and wrapped in cellophane, you'd coo at it like a newborn baby. But my dazzling smile garners no response. Okay.

I don't really care, ("But you've just written a lengthy essay about it, John . . .") I expect nothing, and that's what I get. Perhaps I'm just projecting my self-disgust at the shards of excavated crockery that populated my mouth for so long.

But Susan likes the teeth. Several times a day she'll stop me and ask me to smile, like I was a woman in the street just trying to live her life. When I smile, she smiles back at me, and her smile is my favourite smile. Mine is now my second favourite. So, it *has* all been worthwhile.

I shall miss the Dentist. He was the only person I knew who was really interested in my film career. We were quite pally by the end. Mind you, I'd be very matey if every time I met someone, they gave me a thousand quid. They'd be in my will.

And that's the end of it. First appointment in January, my next and last appointment will be in June. Six months to turn a landfill into an ornamental garden. There are peacocks strutting on my gums. Six months lying on my back with my mouth open, being taken advantage of. Like being back in prison. It's over.

Until I get the implants, obviously.

A GLOSSARY OF TOOTHSOME TERMS

———————◆———————

3 **my pub piano teeth**: A piano was often used as accompaniment for cockney sing-a-longs in British pubs of the past, the white keys sallowing over time because of the perpetual peasouper cigarette smoke. Today the pub piano has been replaced by a bearded young man with an acoustic guitar doing fiercely amplified Coldplay covers, even though nobody wants him to.

6 **David Sylvian**: David Sylvian was the singer of glamorous art-rockers, Japan. He is known for the Princess Diana sweep of his fringe, the dolorous melodrama of his voice and the fact he hasn't aired his teeth in public since 1975.

6 **the Cliff Richard manner**: Cliff Richard is a pop singer and tennis enthusiast, famed in Britain for his youthful good looks, despite the fact he is palpably ancient. Lately interred from an Egyptian tomb ancient. His death is reported each year during the Glastonbury Festival as a prank.

6 **Max Headroom smile**: Max Headroom was a faux-A.I. television presenter briefly fashionable in the 1980s.

6 **Rylan**: Rylan is a British television presenter briefly fashionable right now.

7 **Dot Cotton's plum rinse**: Dot Cotton, played by June Brown, was a character in the British soap *Eastenders*. She was known for looking aghast, smoking heavily and having hair the colour of deep bruising.

12 **George Washington**: George Washington was the first president of the United States of America.

19 **better teeth than our American cousins**: Yeah, but the BRITISH Medical Journal *would* say that, wouldn't it?

23 **a tall Reece Shearsmith, without the rage**: Reece Shearsmith is a British comic actor and writer. He is one quarter of *The League of Gentlemen* and wrote and starred in *Psychoville* and *Inside No 9* with Steve Pemberton. Everything he's done is great. Sickening.

26 **the National Trust**: The National Trust is a charity for heritage conservation in England, Wales and Northern Ireland, founded in 1895. Basically, if it's old, ruined and out of the way, they will charge you to go near it.

34 **lengthy waits in the Dole Office**: The Dole Office is a colloquial term for The Department of Work and Pensions, a building in every town where, in return for getting out of bed in the morning and filling in a book of lies about your attempts to find employment, a stern-faced office worker will give you a small amount of money. It's not their actual money, but they are obliged to act as if it is. In the '60s, '70s and '80s it was possible to live reasonably well off the dole, and it accidentally sponsored most of the rock and pop music the UK gifted the world, acting almost as an arts grant. This is no longer the case.

34 **Lord Sugar**: Alan Sugar (now Baron Sugar) is an unpleasant billionaire and the host of the UK version of *The Apprentice*. The flat, dunderheaded insults he spits at mooncalf entrepreneurs cowering in front of him each week are scripted, as the Baron is now too important to think.

35 **the Mastermind chair**: *Mastermind* is a British televisual institution where contestants sit in a black, leather chair under a spotlight and a man asks them questions about subjects they profess to know about. It's a quiz show pared back to its bare bones. It's been on TV for as long as I've been alive and that's a very long time.

36 **Bono-style wraparounds**: Bono is an Irish pop singer and influencer.

37 **Norman Wisdom**: Sir Norman Wisdom OBE was an English actor famed for frenetic, physical comedy, mawkish songs and a screen persona that bordered on the imbecilic. A hugely popular fixture in British cinemas in the '50s, his 1969 sex comedy *What's Good for the Goose* has been medically prescribed as an emetic.

37 **Peters and Lee specs**: Peters and Lee were a singing duo who won the talent show *Opportunity Knocks* in the early '70s. Lennie Peters, born in Islington in 1931, was blinded one eye at a time, losing the first to a car accident and the second to someone throwing a brick at his head, suggesting Islington was once a rather rougher place than it is today. Poor Lennie.

41 **Spandau Ballet**: Spandau Ballet were an '80s New Romantic band who wore kilts and carried binoculars and honked like geese and existed solely to make Duran Duran look good.

48 **a small Navvy's tent**: A navvy is a labourer employed in the excavation and construction of a road, railway or a canal. The name comes from the builders of the first navigation canals in the 18th Century. Navvy's tents are erected to keep the unending British rain out of newly dug trenches, but realistically it's a place

where the great British worker can smoke and drink tea until the time comes to "look busy".

49   **crafty wheeze on a tight woodbine**: In Britain the woodbine is the common honeysuckle, in North America it's the Virginian creeper (which sounds like an urban legend). But what I'm referring to here is the once popular brand of strong, cheap cigarettes called Woodbines, a top-contending cause of premature death for British army men of both World Wars. Also known as "gaspers", they were often sold as single cigarettes under the counter to children by tobacconists anxious to safeguard the future of their business.

57   **Calvino's short story "The Naked Breast"**: Italo Calvino, author of *If on A Winter's Night a Traveller*, was the archetypal Italian post-modern writer. But he's a lot better than that sounds.

64   **plump for a Pot Noodle**: Pot Noodle is a dehydrated instant noodle snack food, popular with students and bachelors. It is comprised of equal parts woodchip, sawdust and, it turns out, turmeric. Flavours include morel mushroom and oyster, saffron and samphire and frankincense and myrrh.

64   **banana Nesquik yellow**: Nesquik is a brand of food products including breakfast cereals, powdered mixes for flavoured milk, ready to drink products and, unsurprisingly as Nestlé is a Swiss company, fondue fountains. The colours and flavours are actual Pop Art.

70   **my NHS check-up**: The NHS is Great Britain's finest achievement. After the trauma of the Second World War, it was the promise of life, of healing. At its launch it had three core principles: that it meet the needs of everyone. That it be free at the point of delivery. That it be based on clinical need, not ability to pay. This beautiful idea has been systematically dismantled by people pleading it's no longer fit for purpose and proposing an insurance-based model based on the American system. These are the same people who would earn vast amounts of money should such a system be introduced. I love the NHS and will fight to keep it as I haven't got enough money to be sick. I can't afford to be made homeless by haemorrhoids.

74   **The words of Pam Ayres**: Pam Ayres MBE is a British national treasure. Like Peters and Lee, she also came up through *Opportunity Knocks* and went on to be a popular media presence for fifty years, despite the calamitous drawback of being a performance poet. If you can imagine P J Harvey in sensible shoes . . .

75 **Les Dawson shifting his bosom**: Les Dawson, an erudite and serious man, is famous in the UK for playing the piano incorrectly, dressing up as elderly women and saying "Knickers, knockers, knackers", which translates into standard English as "Underwear, breasts, testicles", a less successful catchphrase. Another alumni of the school of *Opportunity Knocks*.

83 **pick up some Steradent from a Pound Shop**: Since the collapse of the British high street—the post offices and newsagents are long gone—replaced by pawnbrokers, tattooists, vape outlets and pound shops. The joy of the pound shop is its simplicity—everything costs a pound. Until you take it to the till, at which point it becomes slightly more than a pound for some reason.

97 **Breville Sandwich maker**: The Breville Sandwich Maker, like the "Pie Iron" or "Waffle Iron" or Iron Man's head, features a popular clamshell design, and is beloved of students and bachelors. It heats, toasts and seals any sandwich, but if that sandwich doesn't have cheese in it there's absolutely no point. You're wasting everybody's time. Cheese is life. Non, je ne rennet rien.

99 **eligible for a bus pass**: In the UK you can apply for a free bus pass at the ripe old age of 66, meaning you get to spend your twilight years standing at bus stops in the pissing rain weighed down by your tins of cat food, staring at a series of cancellations on the "Bus Tracker" FOR FREE.

103 **the painting by Holbein**: *The Ambassadors* by Holbein features an anamorphic skull slatting across the foreground of the picture as a *vanitas*, symbolically showing the transience of life and the futility of pleasure, two things that, in my experience, aren't usually that oblique.

105 **drawing a bead on the Armitage Shanks**: Armitage Shanks are purveyors of "sanitary pottery manufacture" since 1817, and emblematic of comfort, reliability and release nationwide. This is the throne we all kneel before, usually after a heavy Friday night.

106 *Father Ted*: *Father Ted* was a beloved sit-com featuring the adventures of three Irish priests and their housekeeper trapped on a small, inhospitable, wet island and bored out of their minds. Given their vow of chastity too, it stands as a potent metaphor for the UK.

John Patrick Higgins is a writer and director. He lives in Belfast, where it rains.

Printed in the USA
CPSIA information can be obtained
at www.ICGtesting.com
JSHW021716110224
57068JS00003B/206